F. 75¢

THE HERITAGE OF EARLY BRITAIN

THE HERITAGE
OF
EARLY BRITAIN

by

M. P. CHARLESWORTH   M. D. KNOWLES

G. E. DANIEL   P. H. BLAIR

J. G. D. CLARK   NORA K. CHADWICK

J. M. DE NAVARRO   E. MILLER

of

CAMBRIDGE
UNIVERSITY

LONDON

G. BELL AND SONS LTD

1952

TO THE MEMORY OF
MARTIN CHARLESWORTH

Printed in Great Britain by
NEILL & CO. LTD., EDINBURGH

Preface

THIS book had its origin in a course of lectures delivered at Cambridge in the Lent Term of 1949. They were organised by Martin Charlesworth, who conceived the idea of assembling a team from three different faculties to present a composite picture of British prehistory and early history in a way that might appeal to hearers reading a great variety of subjects other than history. The lectures did in fact draw audiences far larger than Charlesworth had expected, and within a few months were broadcast without a great change of content. When, some months later, a proposal for publication in book form was made, there was some hesitation; it was thought that the earlier lectures had in their original form been designed to accompany a series of lantern-slides, while one or two of the other speakers felt that a lecture or a broadcast talk was something different from the chapter of a book. Charlesworth, however, would take no refusal, and his tactful perseverance broke down all resistance. With a modesty and generosity that were characteristic, he insisted on sharing the title of editor with another, and when he was suddenly taken from us it was left to the present writer to draw upon the reserve of goodwill he had created. The book, as it now appears, is a memorial to one side of his activity, and we dedicate it to his memory.

M. D. K.

Cambridge, *March*, 1951

Acknowledgments

PERMISSION has been given for the inclusion of certain copyright material, and grateful acknowledgment is made to the following authors, publishers, collectors and institutions:—

To Sir Ifor Williams for his translation of the medieval Welsh lullaby quoted in chapter V.

To Constable and Company Ltd. and to the representative of the late Kuno Meyer for nine pieces of verse from his *Ancient Irish Poetry* quoted in chapter V.

To the University Museum of Archæology and Ethnology, Cambridge, for Plates 1, 2, 3, 4, 5 and 21.

To the Ordnance Survey and Mr. O. G. S. Crawford, C.B.E., F.B.A., for Plate 8.

To the National Museum of Antiquities, Dublin, for Plate 9.

To Dr. P. Jacobsthal and the Oxford University Press for Plates 11a, 11b, 12a, 13a and 13b, and to the same publishers for three passages from A. W. Wade-Evans' *Welsh Medieval Law* quoted in chapter V.

To the Trustees of the British Museum for Plates 10, 16a, 16c, 22 and 23, and for figs. v and viii.

To Liverpool Public Museum and Mr. E. T. Leeds for Plates 12b and 15a.

To His Grace the Duke of Northumberland for Plate 14.

To the National Museum of Wales for Plate 15b.

To Bedford Modern School Museum and the Royal Society of Antiquaries of London for Plate 16b, and to the same society for fig. iv and fig. vii.

To Mr. G. E. Peachey for Plate 17.

To Dr. J. K. St. Joseph, Curator of Aerial Photography in the University of Cambridge, for Plate 18.

To Mr. Thomas H. Mason of Dublin for Plate 20b.

To B. T. Batsford Ltd. for fig. iii.

To Mr. F. Turner, formerly of Brentford Public Library, for a print of fig. iv.

To the Royal Society of Antiquaries of Ireland for fig. vi.

6

Contents

List of Plates

(following page 196)

LIST OF PLATES

List of Figures

I

G. E. DANIEL

The Peoples of Prehistoric Britain

'SIR,' said Dr. Johnson, 'all that is really known of the ancient state of Britain is contained in a few pages. We can know no more than what old writers have told us.' To Dr. Johnson, then, the early history of Britain began with the first classical literary sources —with Julius Cæsar, Tacitus, Diodorus Siculus, Strabo, and the other writers in Greek and Latin who give us tantalisingly brief and often third-hand accounts of early Britain. The heritage of early Britain, in the sense of a heritage that could be appreciated and described, was to Johnson and his contemporaries something that started with 55 B.C., and with the Roman conquest.

This attitude of mind had come into existence in the seventeenth century, when historians changed from a reliance on oral and imaginary sources for our national origins, and began to place their faith in classical literary sources. They began to give up believing in the Trojan origin of the British, in King Brute, in King Arthur, and the Phœnicians, and to adopt a more sceptical attitude which made British history start with the Romans, the Ancient British and the Druids.

Principal among the seventeenth-century English antiquaries was John Aubrey, and he sets the pattern
for the traditional and pre-archæological picture of
early Britain.   What sort of a country was pre-Roman
Britain, asked Aubrey, and this was his answer: 'a
shady dismal wood, and the inhabitants almost as savage
as the Beasts whose skins were their only rayment.   The
language British, which, for the honour of it, was in
those days spoken from the Orcades to Italie and Spain.
Their religion is at large described by Cæsar.   Their
priests were Druids.   Their way of fighting is lively sett
down by Cæsar.   They knew the use of iron.   They
were two or three degrees I suppose less savage than
the Americans.   The Romans subdued and civilised
them'.

Aubrey's account still has a very familiar ring.   It is so
similar to the brief account with which the school books
of the last hundred and fifty years have opened, passing
after a few paragraphs, with indecent haste and such
obvious relief, to the invasions of Julius Cæsar and the
Romans, which were, after all, history.   Let us take
two typical examples of nineteenth-century history
books: Mrs. Markham's *History of England* and Lady
Calcott's *Little Arthur's History of England*.   'There was
once a time,' wrote Mrs. Markham, in her characteristically agreeable style, 'when there were neither roads
nor bridges nor houses nor churches in Britain.   The
country was nothing but an overgrown forest.   The
people lived in holes in the ground or in any miser-
able huts they could contrive.   Hunting was their chief
employment.   They had war chariots of a very extra-
ordinary kind with sharp scythes fixed in the axletrees
of the wheels which they drove in amongst their
enemies to their great destruction.   They could neither

read nor write nor sew nor weave. What we call education had not as yet made any progress among them, and they have not left us any history of themselves.' So much for Mrs. Markham. *Little Arthur* says much the same thing. 'Britain was so full of trees,' wrote Lady Calcott, 'that there was very little room for houses and still less for cornfields. There were no gardens. In the summer the Britons went naked and instead of clothes they put paint upon their bodies. They were very fond of a fine blue colour which they made of a plant called woad. They stained themselves with it all over so that from a distance they looked as if they were dressed in tight blue clothes.'

I have quoted from Mrs. Markham and Lady Calcott because they are especially entertaining to us at the present day, but the picture they give is typical of the traditional pre-archæological picture that lasts through to the beginning of current school books and to *1066 and All That*. The impenetrable forests, the woad-painted savages, the chariots with their scythes, the Druids cutting mistletoe from the oak-trees—we must admit that this is a picture of the earliest past of Britain which we all have, or have had, in the backs of our minds. What an amusing, simple, and yet totally unreal picture it is. Of course the picture is entirely derived from, and therefore limited by, the written sources in Greek and Latin to which I have already referred. Mrs. Markham and Lady Calcott believed, with Dr. Johnson, that the 'old writers' were the final arbiters of our knowledge of early Britain. That was of course the essence of Mrs. Markham's complaint—the ancient Britons had left us no history of themselves.

It is true that the history of Britain in its strict sense, that is to say, written history, only begins with Cæsar.

In the last hundred years, however, with the great development of archæology, we have realised that before written history there lies the great prehistoric past of man. Indeed it is now clear that written history is only the very last scene in the long drama of man's development. What we call prehistory takes up nearly ninety-nine per cent. of man's life on this earth. For, according to the geologists and geochronologists, the first human tools were made about 600,000 years ago, while the first written records in Egypt and Sumer fairly certainly date from at most 5000 years ago. If we imagine the past of man, or rather his past as attested by surviving tools, as occupying an hour of the clock, then written history has so far only occupied half a minute of human time. Prehistorians are never tired of making these facile comparisons but they should not be misunderstood—prehistory is not necessarily more important than written history because it came first and lasted longer. It would be futile to introduce value concepts into the appraisal of prehistory and history *sensu stricto*. But it is fair to say that nowadays we can only understand the heritage of early Britain by going behind the written sources which limited the historical perspective of Dr. Johnson and Little Arthur, and by studying the pre-Roman people whom archæology has revealed to us.

To do this we must understand the methods and limitations of archæology. Our knowledge of the peoples of pre-Roman Britain at the present day is based on many sources: they include classical literary sources, oral traditions surviving in later native literature, the facts of physical anthropology, the facts of linguistic distribution, survivals in material culture and custom, and, lastly, the material remains of pre-

Roman Britain. It is this last source, the archæological source, which is now our paramount source of information, but its potentialities and value have been widely understood only in the last fifty years, so that the pre-archæological traditional picture still survives, and it was still possible for an historian of great reputation, Sir John Marriott, to write in 1938 in his *The Realm of England*, 'Of the inhabitants of pre-Roman Britain a good deal has of late been written, but little is known.'

This is not the place to discuss the methods by which the prehistorian or the prehistoric archæologist wrests the facts of history from the material remains of man's prehistoric past.[1] But it is the place to stress the limitations of prehistory. The prehistorian has only the material remains of pre-Roman Britain to guide him—the tools, ornaments, houses, tombs. From these he naturally builds up a picture which is mainly, and inevitably, material; he is bound to be concerned in the main with the non-spiritual, non-mental aspects of early British culture. We can then only make guesses at the intangibles of early man in Britain; we often talk loosely of the imperishable ideals of a way of life, and it is a fine phrase. But, alas, from the point of view of prehistoric archæology, it is the ideals which perish, and it is the clay vessels and bronze knives and iron ploughshares that remain. The picture we can then give of our earliest heritage—the pre-Roman period—is thus a lopsided one. We can only guess at the non-material culture of early man by general parallels with existing primitives, and to base any historical theory on these parallels is absurd. Because a prehistoric culture reveals tools very like those of a modern primitive tribe we cannot induce that the prehistoric bearers and creators of that culture practised the same customs, and held the same beliefs, as the modern primitives who have reached the same technological stage. Here we touch on the disappointments of prehistory to the enthusiastic student of man's past; prehistory is anonymous. The architect who planned Stonehenge is nameless, the contractor who moved the blue stones from the Presely Hills to Salisbury Plain is nameless, and nameless too is the man—if there be one—buried in the middle of Silbury Hill. We can say that Stonehenge is a large impressive structure, not obviously a house or a tomb; it is by inference a great ritual centre, perhaps one might say a great magico-religious centre—but if we say more, we are guessing. It is easier to date Stonehenge than to say what went on inside it. True, Stonehenge is, admittedly, orientated to the midsummer sunrise, but then our churches point to the east and Christianity is not sun-worship.

I often think that an archæologist of the future studying the remains of Cambridge, provided he had no inscriptions and written sources to guide him, would go far astray in reconstructing the non-material life of this town. He would without doubt regard the Round Church and St. John's Chapel as the shrines of separate religions, and would argue whether the round-temple plan was earlier or later than the rectangular one. And, faced with the plans of King's Chapel, the Victoria Cinema, and the lecture rooms in Mill Lane, which would he assign as the main cult-shrines of our present culture?

But, despite, and within, these limitations, there are three extremely important aspects of pre-Roman Britain that we can describe. The first is the way in which people gained their livelihood—the economic basis of their life. We can say from archæological evidence whether they were hunter-fishers or pastoralists or agriculturists, what crops they cultivated, what animals they domesticated, what their fields were like, their farms, their crafts, their trade. This economic heritage of early Britain is the subject of the second chapter in this book. The second thing about which we can say something definite regarding Britain in prehistoric times is closely allied to arts and crafts; it is the art of the unlettered savages who lived in England and Wales before Cæsar and Claudius. It still comes as a surprise to some that there was any art in pre-Roman times. Yet art there was, and its claims on us are not that it is the first art, or that it is very old, but that it is beautiful, that it is æsthetically satisfying, and is, indeed, as much an expression of the strivings of the human spirit as the artistic adventures of historic times. I have used the phrase 'the human spirit' advisedly, because in looking at the artistic achievements of early man we do perhaps, for once, get nearer the intangibles than anywhere else in prehistory. The most mannered and, to my mind, the most exciting and satisfying school of art in pre-Roman Britain was that created by the Celts, who lived in England and Wales immediately before the Roman conquest—the people who made the Birdlip mirror and the Battersea shield, and threw into the Llyn Cerrig Bach bog in Anglesey the very remarkable collection of objects recovered during the last war through the chance making of an aerodrome. This school of art—one of the real glories of our pre-Roman heritage—is fully discussed by Mr. de Navarro in the third chapter.[2]

Two things have now been mentioned that are of importance and about which the archæologist of pre-Roman Britain can speak fully and with authority: these we may call the economic and artistic heritages. There is a third heritage—the ethnic and cultural heritage. As we study the archæological remains of early Britain, arranged as they are according to their relations in space and time, we notice at once differences in the record—differences of distribution both in time and space. The differences are due to the arrival of new people with new ways of life, or at least with new forms of material culture. These changes—changes in the form of tools, houses, tombs and temples—are observed carefully by the archæologist. They are the same kinds of changes in material culture that occur in historic times, as when, in the eleventh and twelfth centuries in England, there appeared new forms of ecclesiastical and domestic architecture. We know from written sources that these changes in the eleventh and twelfth centuries were due to the invasion of the Normans; and it therefore seems reasonable to suppose that the sudden and sharp, and often very remarkable, changes in the archæological record in prehistoric times are also due to the invasion of new people with a new culture. But there is this difference in dealing with the assumed prehistoric invasions: we cannot label the invading cultures of pre-Roman Britain with ready-made folk names. We have no names like Saxons or Normans to apply, so that the prehistoric archæologist has to invent names. Some of these names he takes from typical objects of material culture, like beakers or megalithic tombs, or from sites where typical relics are found, like Windmill Hill, or from the area occupied by a new culture, like Wessex or the Cotswold-Severn area. These archæologically labelled, but really anonymous, people of Britain have to be fitted against the general industrial and chronological background of pre-Roman Britain.

The current framework of reference for prehistoric Europe is based on the material used by man for making his tools. From the early days of prehistoric archæology it has been customary to divide man's prehistoric past in Europe into three successive ages, or phases, or technological stages—the Ages of Stone, of Bronze, and of Iron. This framework, based on archæological facts, has now succeeded the idea of Ancient Britons based on the facts in classical literary sources, just as the Ancient Britons succeeded tales of Trojans and Phœnicians and King Arthur based on hypothesis, invention and folk-tale. The first archæologists were mainly geologists and natural scientists, and they treated these three ages as though they were geological epochs, subdividing them into smaller periods. Thus the Stone Age was divided into the Palæolithic or Old Stone Age, the Mesolithic or Middle Stone Age, and the Neolithic or New Stone Age. Then the Bronze Age was divided into an Early, Middle and Late Bronze Age. The Iron Age, of course, belongs to historic as well as prehistoric times, so the prehistoric Iron Age was called the Early Iron Age, and it has been in Europe further divided into two phases, an earlier or Hallstatt phase, and a later or La Tène phase.

This epochal idea of prehistory was, and still is, a useful framework for studying prehistory, but it is very little more. When prehistorians discovered that parts of some of their 'epochs' were contemporary they realised that they were not dealing with periods of time, but with patterns of tools, with assemblages of artifacts which are typical of the material culture of societies, and that, as we have said, these societies had to be conceived of both spatially and temporally. Under the influence of the German culture-historical school, and dazzled by the way in which classical prehistorians were talking of Ægean, Mycenæan and Minoan civilisations, the students of pre-Roman Britain have begun to abandon the old epochal idea of prehistory and to think in terms of the material cultures of these social groups. But while the description of our heritage from the culture of these anonymous prehistoric societies is one of the aims of the prehistoric archæologist, we still have to retain the old epochal divisions as the most convenient framework for our story of pre-Roman Britain.

Set out here are the conventional dates for these epochal subdivisions in southern Britain. At the same time, for a general picture of the cultural elements in the heritage of pre-Roman Britain we can best think of this long story as falling into four major phases: (I) the phase corresponding to the Lower and Middle Palæolithic, (II) the phase corresponding to the Upper Palæolithic and Mesolithic, (III) the phase corresponding to the Neolithic and the Early and Middle Bronze Ages, which coincides very approximately with the second

Phase I	Lower Palæolithic Middle Palæolithic	*c.* 600,000 B.C. to 30,000 B.C.
Phase II	Upper Palæolithic Mesolithic	30,000 B.C. to 2,000 B.C.
Phase III	Neolithic Age Early Bronze Age Middle Bronze Age	*c.* 2,000 B.C. to 1,700 B.C. 1,700 B.C. to 1,400 B.C. 1,400 B.C. to 1,000 B.C.
Phase IV	Late Bronze Age Early Iron Age	1,000 B.C. to 400 B.C. 400 B.C. to 43 A.D.

millennium B.C., and (IV) the phase corresponding to the Late Bronze Age and the Early Iron Age which coincides approximately with the first millennium B.C. These dates are, of course, only very approximate and in any case could only be said to apply with any force to south-eastern Britain.

Let us now take a glance at the ethnic and cultural elements that existed in Britain in these various periods.[3] The Lower and the Middle Palæolithic are the times that we know least about. This first phase of British history begins with the first archæological appearance of man as attested by simple stone tools, at the beginning of what the geologists call the Pleistocene period—the period of the Quaternary Ice Age—at a time which, as we have seen, the geochronologists place some 600,000 years ago. The Pleistocene was not a period of continuous cold; it was divided into four major cold periods—the maxima of the ice advances, separated by three interglacial periods when the climate of Britain was warmer than at present. Throughout the long millennia of the Pleistocene, Britain did not exist as a separate island; the British Islands as they now are were part of the continent of Europe.

The first of man's tools that have survived are simple flakes and cores of flint—the so-called dawnstones or eoliths, and it is inevitable that these earliest tools should have been the subject of great controversy. It will always be difficult to recognise with certainty the first stone tools fashioned by man and we should here also remember that there may have been a tool-using phase in man's past before the first stone tools— a Palæoxylic Age in fact before the Palæolithic, when man's tools were of wood. Of such an age we are likely ever to remain ignorant; indeed here we again meet the fundamental difficulty of prehistoric archæ-ology—the limitations imposed on our historical narrative by the different rate of survival of man's cultural remains. All we can say with certainty is that gradually stone tools are found of the authenticity of which there is no doubt, and that, when we come across the fine hand-axes and worked flints characteristic of the Lower and Middle Palæolithic, we are really in the presence of the tools of the first British societies about which we have certain knowledge.

Of the actual people who made these first tools in this first phase of our early story we know next to nothing. At Swanscombe in Kent was found the skull of one of the makers of the early hand-axes, and he has every right to be called the First Englishman. This title was originally bestowed by Sir Arthur Keith on the Piltdown remains—*Eoanthropus Dawsonii*—but the early date of Piltdown has now been disproved by the fluorine test.

The second phase of British prehistory began not earlier than the last glaciation some 20,000 to 30,000 years ago, and lasts to the end of the third millennium. It corresponds to the Upper Palæolithic and Mesolithic of the earlier systematists. The Upper Palæolithic industries are well represented in France—their stone tools are mainly blades of flint, and their tools were much smaller and finer than those of the earlier phase; their makers are men whom the physical anthro-pologists definitely class as *Homo sapiens*, they practised careful or ceremonial burial, which may or may not indicate a belief in the after-life, and they had a most remarkable mural and portable art. The Upper Palæo-lithic food-gatherers followed the reindeer, mammoth and woolly rhinoceros across the land-bridge to Britain. We know of them from their tools, but unfortunately we have no British examples of their magnificent cave and home art; our only examples of this first flowering of man's artistic genius are a few pieces of crudely engraved bone from rock-shelters in Derbyshire. We have however from Britain a good example of the ceremonial burial of this phase—the burial of a tall man of about twenty-five years of age in the cave of Paviland on the Gower peninsula—the so-called Red Lady of Paviland. The Mesolithic industries which succeed the Upper Palæolithic in Britain show two tendencies, the first a tendency to the production of very small flints— microliths as they are called, and the second the making of heavy wood-cutting tools for dealing with the new forests in which man found himself as the ice-sheets of the last glaciation finally withdrew. The hunters and fishers of the Mesolithic period might be called the first inhabitants of the British Isles, as distinct from their Palæolithic predecessors who had lived on the fringe of the European mainland. The separation of Britain from the continent had taken place by about 4,000 B.C.—perhaps somewhere between six and eight thousand years ago.

The Mesolithic hunter-fishers, who lived in small nomadic communities during the millennia that separate the end of the last ice age from the first appearance of peasant village agriculturists, form the first basic element in our ethnic and cultural heritage. There were probably very few people in Britain in these first two phases of her history; indeed from both phases we still have little more than a dozen skeletons. It has been estimated by J. G. D. Clark that the population of Britain in Mesolithic times was about 250, and while such a number must always remain a matter of guesswork, it probably does not err on the large side. The contribution, therefore, of the Mesolithic hunter-fishers to British history cannot be great. They survived into the next phase, and learnt the arts of agriculture and domestication of animals from the Neolithic invaders. Their physical heritage may survive; indeed Professor Fleure has distinguished Upper Palæolithic strains in the modern population of West Wales, but practically nothing survives of their cultural heritage—unless it be the arts of hunting and fishing.

At the time when Britain was becoming an island, say 6,000 or more years ago, the Mesolithic food-gatherers in the Near East made several discoveries revolutionary to human life. The two most important of these were the cultivation of grain and the domestication of animals. These discoveries form the basis of what has been called the Food-Producing or Neolithic Revolution in human history, and they spread slowly over the old world. They reached Britain about 2,000 B.C. Our first Neolithic villagers were the Windmill Hill people, who settled mainly in southern Britain somewhat before 2,000 B.C. And soon after, the prehistoric archæologist distinguishes other groups of pastoralists and agriculturists: the Peterborough and Skara Brae people in the east and north, the builders of chambered tombs—the so-called Megalithic People—mainly in western Britain and Ireland, and various different groups of people, whose characteristic pottery drinking vessel, buried with their dead, has given them the name of the Beaker peoples (see Plates 1 and 2). The knowledge of metallurgy, in existence in the Near East in the fourth millennium, began to spread among these earliest peasant village communities in the period from 1700 to 1400 B.C., and tools of copper and bronze begin to appear. The British bronze industry derived its inspiration partly from Central Europe and partly from Spain; its earliest triumphs were in Ireland, but gradually the centre of gravity changed to southern England. The industry was given its great fillip by the arrival in Wessex about 1500 to 1400 B.C. of folk from Brittany—the people of the so-called Wessex culture, who brought with them skilled bronze-smiths and goldsmiths.

It was these anonymous people of the first half of the second millennium B.C., now bearing these various archæological labels, who brought to Britain in diluted and transmuted form the elements of civilisation which were being developed in the Near East in the fourth and third millennia B.C. It now seems most unlikely that there was at this time any direct connection between Britain and the ancient civilisations of the Near East, and so the Egyptians, Phœnicians, Cretans and Israelites with whom some wayward scholars have peopled prehistoric Britain must be set down as the products of imagination, not archæology.

The arrival of the Wessex folk is the last of the invasions of prehistoric Britain that took place in our Phase III. The rest of this phase—the period which in archæological parlance is the Middle Bronze Age—is one of assimilation, of the transmutation of these new cultural elements into a native British culture or civilisation (see Plate 3): the first time in her history when Britain can be said to have a cultural individuality. After three or four hundred years, changes took place which initiated and spanned the fourth phase we have distinguished in British prehistory, the period convention-ally known as the Late Bronze Age and Early Iron Age.

The changes began with the use of new types of bronze implements (see Plate 4), new forms of agriculture (see Plate 8) and the burial of the dead cremated in urnfields. From some of their urnfields, these Late Bronze Age invaders have been called the Deverel-Rimbury folk, but these folk are only one of the constituent elements in many separate groups that came to England in the first half of the first millennium B.C.—groups from Switzerland, the Low Countries, and from France.

The extensive use of iron was first known probably to the Hittites in Asia Minor about the fourteenth century B.C. In Europe the first iron-using culture developed in south Austria soon after 1000 B.C. and is known from its type site there as the Hallstatt culture. Iron-using folk of Hallstatt tradition invaded southern Britain in the fifth century B.C., forming the Iron Age A group or culture, so named by Professor Hawkes. Among the Hallstatt folk of the Middle Rhine, foreign influences from the Greeks in south France, from the Etruscans in Italy, and perhaps even from the Scyths, produced a native barbarian civilisation—if such a phrase is permissible—labelled by archæologists that of La Tène. Invasions of La Tène folk in the third and second centuries B.C. produced in Britain the Iron Age B cultures of Hawkes. Finally came the last in this catalogue of invasions: about 75 B.C. a modified La Tène culture was introduced into south-east Britain from the Ardennes region, forming the Iron Age C culture of Hawkes. These Late Bronze Age and Iron Age invasions form the second great series of folk movements into prehistoric Britain, and Hawkes has very aptly called it the Heroic Age of prehistoric Britain.[4]

We have spoken of the two series of invasions which built the ethnic heritage of early Britain—those of the first half of the second millennium, and those of the heroic age of prehistoric Britain. Invasions they certainly were in the sense of cultural innovations; they represent breaks in the archæological record and the appearance of new forms of material culture, but how formative they were from the ethnic point of view is most difficult to assess. Are we to interpret every group of archæological novelties as due to an 'invasion'? The Windmill Hill folk were almost certainly ordinary settlers, and so probably were the Skara Brae people; but the Peterborough folk may be no more than groups of Mesolithic hunter-fishers who assimilated some of the elements of a post-Mesolithic economy from neighbouring peoples. The builders of the megalithic tombs have suffered from a wealth of speculative interpretation—they have been called traders, missionaries, travelling undertakers: to me they have a reasonable chance of being ordinary colonists looking for somewhere to live and perhaps sources of metal ore. The Beaker folk have been called pastoral aristocrats and the Wessex folk warrior chieftains—and there is good evidence for both interpretations. It also seems likely that the novelties in bronze types which initiated the Late Bronze Age—the socketed axe, the slashing sword and the spearhead—were introduced by travelling smiths and not by folk invasions; certainly there appears in the Late Bronze Age the so-called Founder's Hoard (see Plate 4), with its broken metal, misfits and slag which suggest the stock-in-trade of the travelling smith. We cannot then be certain of the size and nature of the various intrusive elements that make up our book of prehistoric invasions. We can admittedly point to the two periods when pre-Roman Britain was in the main peopled, but we cannot give any estimate of the relative importance of the various elements ethnically; nor can we say whether, for example, in any particular instance where an archæological invasion is attested in prehistorical times, it is the invader or the native elements that triumphed. The mechanics of cultural diffusion are various and complex, as can be very readily seen if thought is given to an invasion such as the Norman one in Britain of which we have both archæological and literary evidence. The same complexity and doubt exists in studying protohistoric invasions like those of the Anglo-Saxons into Britain, and the Britons into Brittany. The archæological record is thin and silent on many aspects of the invasions, and the literary sources of little more help. If we cannot tell with any certainty the nature of the Anglo-Saxon invasion, how much less likely are we to know with any certainty the nature of the prehistoric invasions postulated on the dramatic breaks in the archæological record?

While we cannot be certain about the size and nature of the various invading elements in the ethnic heritage of pre-Roman Britain, we cannot label them with names other than the unfamiliar archæological labels— with one exception. The Iron Age C folk are the Belgæ, and we may refer to that last prehistoric invasion of Britain as the Belgic invasion.[5] But we cannot give linguistic or national labels to any of the other peoples who go by archæological or geographical labels. It used to be the fashion to label the Neolithic folk as Iberians (or even Picts), the Bronze Age folk as Goidels —speakers of the Q-Celtic languages which survive in Erse and Scots Gaelic, and the Early Iron Age folk as Brythons—speakers of the P-Celtic tongues which survive in Welsh and Breton. In fact the names

Goidel and Brython were invented by Sir John Rhys for the speakers of the Q- and P-Celtic languages. (Rhys's *Celtic Britain* was published in 1882; *The Welsh People*, which he wrote with D. Brynmor Jones, in 1900.) They are widely used in archæological literature from 1900 to the 1930s. However these were fashions of a day which did not appreciate the complexity of the archæological record, nor the strange ways in which languages spread and change. Little useful purpose can be served by guessing which of the various prehistoric invaders spoke which language. Yet we can say with some certainty that it is most unlikely the Windmill Hill folk, and the builders of the megalithic tombs, spoke an Indo-European language; they probably spoke languages akin to those that flourished in the Mediterranean before the arrival of the Indo-European speakers. We can also say with some certainty that most of the invaders of the heroic age of British prehistory in the Late Bronze Age and Early Iron Age spoke varieties of languages which ultimately gave rise to the Q- and P-Celtic tongues of history.

It is also extremely difficult to make equations between the archæological invasions and the facts of physical anthropology. It is obvious that the invasions from western Europe brought to our shores more members of the Mediterranean race type than did invasions from the Low Countries and Germany. To a certain extent it is still possible to make statements like that of Sir O. M. Edward in Traill's *Social History* when he declares the Neolithic people period in Wales was due to 'a wave of men of short stature and of swarthy countenance, whose poorest descendants may be seen among the miners of the Rhondda valley or the quadrangles of Jesus College, Oxford', but they are, for the most part, dangerous statements. We have only the skeletons of the pre-Roman Britons, and those only when the last rites were not cremation but burial in the ground; and even such skeletal remains as we have still await complete analysis in exact relation to the archæological record.[6]

It should be stressed here that the prehistory of Britain set out in this introductory chapter, briefly and baldly, as a succession of anonymous invasions, is only one way of looking at our earliest history. Unless we assume that every invasion meant the total destruction of the previous inhabitants—and everything is against this view—then the true story is one of the gradual modifications of prehistoric British culture by the fusion of native and imported elements. The real heritage of this earliest phase in our history is thus the gradual growth of an insular cultural tradition. We see this very clearly during that period of three or four hundred years at the end of the second millennium B.C., when we were for a time free from invasions. This period is the Middle Bronze Age of the archæologists. During that time was forged in southern Britain a native civilisation—we should use no weaker word to describe it—which is the first of our national glories; the first proud page in our island prehistory to which we look back. We see it now in the bronze tools and gold ornaments that survive (Plate 5), and in the magnificent ritual sites like Stonehenge and Avebury. The French can look back in their national heritage to the magnificent painted and engraved caves of Font de Gaume and Combarelles and Lascaux. Our earliest glory is that period at the end of the second millennium B.C., when elements borrowed from western, central and northern Europe were fused into the first native British civilisation.

As it seems to me, the word *heritage* can mean two things: it can mean the things that survive to the present day, or it can mean those things in the past to which we look back with pride or shame as formative or characteristic factors in our past. In both senses of the word, our heritage begins in pre-Roman times.

Even the extreme non-archæological view of history admits that the first component in the British nation is the ancient Britons—'what old writers have told us'; we have seen very briefly here what a complicated ethnic inheritance those ancient Britons described by Cæsar really had. And it is not only ethnic survival of which we speak, when we talk of the earliest heritage of Britain. Our heritage is no less clear in the other sense of the word: it is a superficial, but still widespread view of history which regards it as beginning with, say, Bede and King Alfred—a view which has failed to assimilate a hundred years and more of archæological research, and is therefore very little better than Dr. Johnson's and Little Arthur's view. We must lift our eyes to the abiding prehistoric past which gave us, among other things, the art of the La Tène Celts, and the temples, tombs and craftsmanship of the second millennium B.C. It does, of course, require a very great exercise of historical imagination to clothe the facts of archæology with the semblance of everyday life, but that effort must be made, for it is here, in pre-Roman archæology, that our national heritage begins.

NOTES

1. For an account of these methods see Sir Leonard Woolley, *Digging Up the Past*, 1930 (also in Pelican Books, 1937); J. G. D. Clark, *Archæology and Society*, 1939, 2nd ed. revised, 1947; R. J. C. Atkinson, *Field Archæology*, 1946.

2. For a general discussion of early British Art see Piggott and Daniel, *A Picture Book of Ancient British Art* (Cambridge, 1951).

3. This is necessarily a very brief account. For fuller treatment see Hawkes and Hawkes, *Prehistoric Britain* (Pelican Books, 1943), also revised and enlarged edition, 1947; J. Hawkes, *Early Britain* (Britain in Pictures Series), 1945; J. G. D. Clark, *Prehistoric England*, 1940, 4th ed. 1948; S. Piggott, *British Prehistory* (Home University Library), 1949; V. G. Childe, *The Prehistoric Communities of the British Isles*, 1940, 3rd ed. 1949.

4. For Professor Hawkes's division of the Early Iron Age in Britain see his article on 'Hill Forts', in *Antiquity*, v (1931).

5. On the Belgic settlements see Hawkes and Dunning, The 'Belgæ of Gaul and Britain,' *Archæological Journal*, lxxxvii (1931).

6. On the relation of the facts of physical anthropology to prehistoric archæology see C. S. Coon, *The Races of Europe* (1939), and Fleure, *The Races of England and Wales* (1923).

II

GRAHAME CLARK

How the Earliest Peoples Lived

THE purpose of this chapter is to consider in broad outline how the prehistoric Britons did not simply manage to survive, but how they raised their standards of living from those of primeval savages to those of the peoples who encountered and were not always conquered by the Roman legions.

The story really falls into two chapters: one immensely long, yet in all essentials monotonous; the other much shorter (though still longer than the whole of British history since the Claudian conquest), but packed with incident and instinct with change.

The abiding wonder of the Old Stone Age is that our forebears survived at all. Physically inferior to many other mammals, scattered sparsely over immense tracts of country, and confronting the elemental forces of nature in small groups, comprising probably not more than ten or fifteen individuals, women and children included, and equipped with a store of knowledge and equipment of frightening inadequacy, they yet fashioned and upheld through thousands of generations the earliest traditions of the human race. During the Pleistocene period vast ice-sheets waxed and waned;

ocean levels rose and fell; animal and plant life underwent successive changes as temperate alternated with glacial phases of climate; yet through it all the men of the Old Stone Age held on and with infinite slowness progressed, thanks alone to the size and quality of their brains, and to their ability through speech to accumulate the results of experience and to transmit cultural traditions.

In this age-long experience we may detect the only inheritance common to all mankind and one which, though overlaid by later and from a chronological point of view quite shallow accretions, plays a greater part in determining human conduct than is always appreciated, or at least admitted, in civilised society.

Through all this primal stage in the evolution of our cultural life the possibilities of existence were narrowly circumscribed by the exigencies of the search for food. Hunting, fishing, fowling and the gathering of eggs, insects and plant products were the only means of obtaining food, and absorbed the main energies of every man, woman and older child in the community. Man was still a parasite living on what he could capture or gather from the animal or plant world about him, not adding to the wealth of nature but merely diverting what he could to his own uses.

During the half-million years or so of their existence as food-gatherers, the kinds of animals and plants on which our earliest ancestors depended underwent profound changes, and this must in itself have called for many readjustments in economic life. There is also evidence, though, for some increase both in the range of food-stuffs and in the efficiency with which these were secured. Although the simian precursors of man were primarily vegetarian in diet, the evidence from Chou-kou-tien in China shows that even the pre-human *Sinanthropus* lived largely on meat; it would appear that it was as a hunter that man first rose to predominance. The hunters of Lower and Middle Palæolithic times would seem to have depended largely on such primitive devices as fall-traps and snares. There is evidence that they used fire-hardened wooden spears, but it was not until Upper Palæolithic times that we meet in the cave deposits with spears and harpoons tipped with flint, antler or bone, or indeed that these latter materials were worked at all into implements or weapons. Again, it is from this period that the first definite traces occur of fishing and fowling, the fishing carried on by lines and gorges, as well possibly as by spears and traps, the fowling mainly by snares.

The equipment of the Mesolithic peoples who continued to support life by food-gathering during the first five thousand years or so of the Post-glacial temperate period in north-western Europe was more elaborate: the bow became more important in this latitude, while hooks, drag-nets and basket weels came into use. Coastal settlement, with marine hunting and fishing, seems also to have begun at this time, though, owing no doubt to the submergence of the ancient coasts, it is only from the end of the period that we first meet with definite evidence of this in Britain, notably in the middens of the Obanians in western Scotland. The middens themselves testify to the importance of shell-fish in the diet of these people, who also hunted seals and caught, presumably from skin boats off-shore, such fish as haddock, common sea-bream, ballan wrasse, thornback ray, skate and a number of sharks. The frequent discovery under the carse clays of the Firth of Forth of the skeletons of rorquals associated with dear-antler axes shows that the Mesolithic folk also took advantage of the larger whales stranded on their shores.

Yet, though it is possible to note some intensification of catching activities, the fact remains that so long as subsistence was based solely on these, the possibilities of social life were severely limited. For one thing, extensive territories were needed to support even a few souls. This meant in practice that communities were limited in size, and even so that they were normally compelled to move with the seasons and gather their food wherever, in the course of nature, it became available. The earliest habitations of which traces have yet been found in Britain are the caves and rock-shelters in the Carboniferous limestones of North and South Wales, of the Wye Valley and Mendips, the Devonian limestone of the Torquay area and the Permian limestone of Creswell Crags, Derbyshire (see Plate 6). Such were occupied at intervals, probably in the main during the winter months, by small bands of Upper Palæolithic hunters. During the summer migrations it is likely that skin tents, supported on poles and weighted by stones round the bottom, were erected in the open. When the glaciers melted the margins of the lakes so formed made attractive camping-places during the warmer part of the year, as the recent excavations at Seamer, Yorkshire, have shown. Elsewhere—as at Farnham, Surrey, and Selmeston, Sussex —there existed traces of light hutments with floors scooped out of the subsoil, but nowhere is there evidence from Mesolithic Britain of organised communities living in substantial houses.

Preoccupation with the bare necessity of maintaining

life, combined with the small size of social groups, set narrow limits to the subdivision of labour and consequently to any notable advances in technology. While one can admire some of the handiwork of our Palæolithic and Mesolithic forebears—the craftsmanship and finish of some of their burins and spearheads, for instance, compare with the luxury products of our modern age—the fact remains that they were limited in their use of organic materials by the potentialities of flint and stone tools, and that metallurgy and a whole series of specialised crafts were still far beyond their reach (see Plate 7).

The circle of savagery was therefore to some degree a closed one, the mode of subsistence limiting the possibility of advances in technique by means of which the primary wants of society might more easily be satisfied. It might be held that the savage state was a prison from which our forebears struggled vainly for long ages to escape, but it would probably be nearer the mark to suggest that, within its own limits, life based on hunting, fishing and gathering was far too satisfying for any such idea to enter the head of Palæolithic or Mesolithic man. He would indeed be a fanatical believer in the virtues of material complexity who, face to face with the Lascaux cave-paintings, could say that the hunters of bison, horse and reindeer were sorry for themselves or their state; or that could they have glimpsed the future they would have pined for the shackles of the farmer or the squalid life of cities.

On the other hand, it is sure enough that the whole history of mankind for good or ill depended on the adoption of a radically new attitude towards external nature: the old parasitical, predatory outlook had to give place to a sustained effort to master natural forces and harness them to the needs of human society. Precisely how, when and where early man first learnt the arts of animal and plant husbandry need not be discussed here. The main point to remember is that, as with Europe as a whole, the new form of economy reached Britain from outside and to a large extent was brought in by actual migration of people. Indeed, it may be emphasised that urban societies had already begun to record their dynastic history in the Nile valley and in parts of western Asia before even a grain of corn was sown on British soil. We were very much on the margin of the ancient world, so that changes accomplished in the Near East affected our economy much later. The fact remains that the Neolithic farmers, who began to colonise Britain rather more than four thousand years ago, were pioneers of civilisation there. Their culti-vated crops and their flocks and herds transformed the basis of subsistence and made possible the comparatively advanced societies of later prehistory.

It should always be remembered, though, that over north-western Europe as a whole the change was not only retarded but gradual. Farming did not so much sweep away as supplement the older ways of obtaining food. It was not merely that groups of hunter-fishers maintained themselves for some time after the immigra-tion of the farmers. The farmers themselves continued to hunt and to fish, to gather plant food and to collect shellfish and eggs. The rhythm of life continued to be set by the seasons, as it still is—more perhaps than we always realise. The activities of the farmer's year were dovetailed into those of the hunter-fisher's: crops, whether sown or wild, were gathered in their season, and the activities of the chase alternated with those of the farm. Indeed, one natural harvest—the hunting of sea-mammals, of whales and seals—was first exploited on a substantial scale by farmers, and has only been developed fully to meet the needs of town-dwellers during modern times. Whales, for instance, were keenly sought by the Iron Age broch and wheel-house people of Caithness, Orkney and the Hebrides, and it is instructive to note that the latter used mattock-blades of whale-rib identical in form with those now employed by the Eskimo for detaching blubber. Yet, although the old catching and gathering activities continued and still continue to provide important sources of food and raw materials, it was farming which broadened the whole basis of feeding and opened up new possibilities for life in early Britain.

When the Neolithic colonisers arrived from the European mainland they found the country still mainly covered by forest, in the lowlands chiefly oak, elm, lime and alder. Farming had in very fact to be carried on at the expense of the forest: from the forest both meadows and cultivated fields had ultimately to be created, possibly the most striking illustration of what was implied in the new outlook. In the clearance of forest two main stages may be distinguished, one prehistoric, the other medieval. In the former the lighter, more easily worked soils, such as gravels and sands, chalk and limestone, and later the intermediate loams were taken in. The heavier claylands were not extensively cleared until early medieval times, but with this we are not concerned here. During the prehistoric period itself two stages can be noted, one in which agriculture was of an extensive shifting character, the other marked by the use of the plough and the cultivation of definite fields.

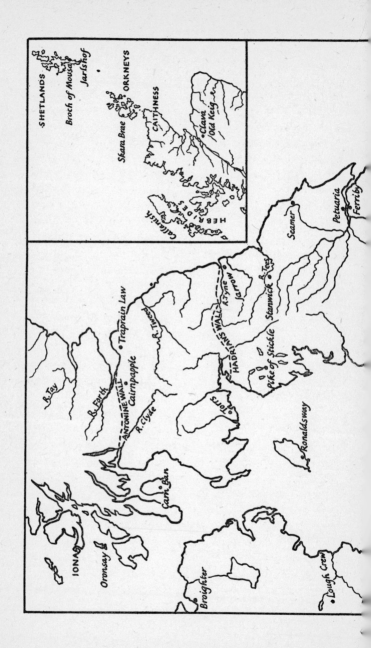

SHETLANDS
Broch of Mousa
Jarlshof

ORKNEYS
Skara Brae

CAITHNESS

Clava
Old Keig

HEBRIDES

Callanish

Petuaria
Ferriby

Seamer

R. Tees
Jarrow
R. Tyne
Stanwick
HADRIAN'S WALL
Pike of Stickle

Traprain Law
R. Tweed

R. Tay
R. Forth
ANTONINE WALL
Cairnpapple
R. Clyde
Torrs

Ronaldsway

IONA
Oronsay
Carn Ban

Broighter
Lough Crew

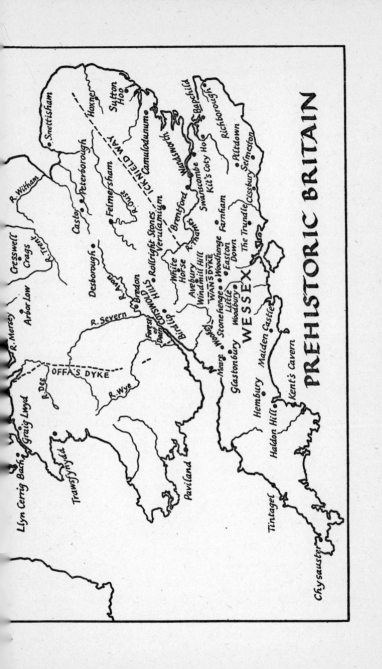

PREHISTORIC BRITAIN

R. Mersey • Cresswell Crags • R. Witham

Llyn Cerrig Bach • Graig Lwyd • Arbor Low • R. Trent

R. Dee • Trawsfynydd • R. Wye

OFFA'S DYKE

Paviland • Forest of Dean • COTSWOLD HILLS • Bredon • R. Avon • Bird Lip

R. Severn

Tintagel • Haldon Hill • Kent's Cavern • Hembury • Maiden Castle • Glastonbury • Meare • Woodbury • Stonehenge • Little Woodbury • Easton • Woodhenge • Farnham

WESSEX

WANSDYKE • Avebury • Windmill Hill • White Horse • Verulamium • Rollright Stones

Desborough • Caston • Peterborough • R. Ouse • Felmersham

Snettisham • Sutton Hoo • Hoxne

ICKNIELD WAY • Camulodunum

Brentford • R. Thames • Swanscombe • Kit's Coty Ho. • Wansworth • Harpchild • Richborough • Pilldown • Selmeston

The Trundle • Cissbury

Chysauster

The earliest phase of British agriculture was essentially one of cutting down and using up forests. The methods used for clearing the ground were felling and burning— the burning was especially important because it provided a top-dressing of potash, so valuable as a fertiliser. Only small areas were dealt with at a time, and from these successive crops were taken until the yield declined. When this happened a new patch would be cleared. This process of clearing, cultivating and shifting to new ground could continue only so long as the forests on the primary soils were able to renew themselves. Inevitably there must have come a time when pressure of population speeded up the process of clearance to a point at which the forest ceased to be able to grow up again fast enough—one must remember, too, that all the while domestic animals worked against the forest by grazing off the seedlings of the trees. So the whole cycle of the clearance and re-growth of the forests broke down. This must have happened earlier in some areas than in others, but everywhere the crisis is likely to have made itself felt during the Bronze Age.

Precisely when fixed fields began to be cultivated in Britain by means of the ox-drawn plough remains obscure. The earliest traces yet recognised are those on the chalk downs of southern England dating from the Late Bronze Age, but it has always to be remembered that traces of still earlier cultivation on more fertile soils may long since have been ploughed away. The ploughs introduced to Britain resembled some wooden ones still to be seen at work round the Mediterranean, and the technique of cultivation itself, involving pulverisation of the soil, was also of Mediterranean origin. The cross-ploughing by which this was effected gave rise to comparatively short, broad fields, the so-called 'Celtic fields' of the downs of Sussex and of Wessex (see Plate 8). When the heavier, intermediate loams began to be taken into cultivation, as they did in the Belgic territories of the south-east towards the end of the prehistoric Iron Age, at a time of heavy rainfall, a new technique of cultivation became necessary, but almost all traces of the longer fields associated with this have been obliterated by nearly two thousand years of subsequent cultivation.

The earliest crops grown in Britain were wheat and barley, but oats, rye and beans were added during the Early Iron Age. The grain was harvested with a saw-like motion by reaping-knives or sickles, which to begin with were armed with flint cutting-edges, either formed from a single piece of flint or from several flakes placed edge to edge. During the period of Sub-Atlantic climate, when rainfall was heavy (if not before), it was common practice to roast the grain before grinding it to flour. This latter process was accomplished in the primitive saddle-quern, in which an upper bolster or rubbing-stone was worked up and down the heavy lower stone. It was not until quite late in the Early Iron Age that the rotary hand-mill, a portable version of the classical donkey-mill adapted by the Roman legionaries and diffused by them over barbarian Europe, reached Britain.

Although we can hardly tell exactly how important agriculture and stock-raising were in relation to one another during prehistoric times, it seems reasonably sure that the earliest husbandry was mixed in character. Before much progress had been made with forest clearance the most important farm animals were cattle and pigs, both able to feed on foliage or mast, except in areas like the Orkney Islands, where trees were scanty and sheep were able to graze on open grassland and on the seashore. As the area of open country expanded in the course of the Bronze Age, sheep and goats came more and more into the picture. By the end of this period also the small Celtic pony, which was to play a striking rôle drawing the chariots of La Tène chieftains, was being bred here. At the time of the heavy increase in rainfall, towards the end of the prehistoric period, there is some evidence for a change from mixed to predominantly pastoral farming in the highland zone of Britain and in Ireland.

During the opening phase of shifting agriculture, settlement was not as permanent as it was later to become, but there is evidence for quite large farms even among Neolithic communities. Much the most complete picture is that given by the villages of Skara Brae and Rinyo on Orkney, where the absence of timber and the nearness of suitable stone caused men to put up buildings which have survived, even down to their internal fittings. The single-roomed houses, rectangular in plan but with rounded corners, had thick walls with dry-stone facings, the inner facing being corbelled so as to overhang appreciably the chamber and thus reduce the area to be roofed over with whalebone and turf. A striking feature of the furnishing of the interiors was their similarity one with another. Each house had a central hearth, and the normal plan was to have beds on either side, with quite an elaborate dresser opposite the entrance, recesses in the thickness of the walls to hold possessions, and stone-lined limpet boxes in one corner. Two main phases of building are recognisable at Skara Brae; in the later of these there were eight houses linked together by stone-lined

Fig. i. Skara Brae, Orkney. Interior of neolithic house, showing stone dresser, central hearth and beds on either side.

passages and ultimately consolidated into an irregular mound through the accumulation of rubbish. Although the Orkney sites give us so clear an impression, it ought always to be remembered that conditions on these northern islands were quite special. Information about Neolithic homesteads in the various parts of Britain must await further exploration. Already, though, it is significant that excavations at localities as far apart as Easton Down (Wilts), Haldon Hill (Devon) and Ronaldsway, on the Isle of Man, have revealed traces of quite substantial rectangular houses, more akin to those still occupied by peasants in outlying parts of Europe than to the primitive shelters of Mesolithic Britain.

Much too little is known about the Bronze Age settlements of Britain, but the earth and stone-walled huts of Dartmoor were round in plan, as were the houses associated with the earliest Celtic fields on the Sussex Downs. The round house indeed, in a great variety of forms, was dominant throughout the rest of British prehistory. In the lowlands the houses were built as a rule of timber and wattle, and some of these were quite substantial. For instance, the later house at the Little Woodbury farmstead near Salisbury, with its central hearth enclosed by a setting of powerful uprights for supporting the tallest portion of the roof, and surrounded by two circles of posts for carrying the lower slopes, was about 45 feet in diameter, large enough to shelter livestock as well as the farmer's family, and possibly servants too.

Two distinct kinds of structure have been found in highland Britain. On the one hand there is the single-roomed house, sometimes having striking regional characteristics, such as the wheel-houses and brochs of north Scotland and the islands, the first with radial stone-built piers in place of an inner circle of posts, and the brochs having cells and spiral staircases in the exaggerated thickness of their walls.   On the other hand there is the type in which the dwelling itself, as well as ancillary compartments like cattle-stalls, is incorporated in a thick curvilinear wall enclosing a courtyard. Such courtyard houses appeared at Jarlshof on Shetland as early as in a local Late Bronze Age context, but in Cornwall, as at Chysauster, they seem not to be older than the latter part of the Early Iron Age, and in North Wales they have been referred to the mid-Roman period.

Even in the more strongly agricultural zones the commonest type of settlement was not the 'British Village' of the old Ordnance Survey maps, but the single farmstead with dwelling and attendant granaries and drying frames, like that at Little Woodbury.   Yet there is some evidence for settlements gathered round a nucleus.   Concentrations of dwellings in hill-forts may in some cases be due to farmers assembling from isolated homesteads to take shelter behind the defences during times of stress; though from the later stages of such a site as Maiden Castle, Dorset, one has the impression rather of more permanently organised settlements.   It might also be said, with a certain truth, that the villages of Glastonbury (which has around sixty huts) and Meare were set in marshes for security, yet the indications of settled village life are quite overwhelming;   the finds, indeed, show that the sites were important centres of village industries, notably leather-working, basket-making, wood-turning and weaving.   In the highland zone, again, court-yard houses were grouped in small hamlets, those at

Chysauster being arranged in pairs on either side of a street.

Although the earliest British farmers lived at a time when metallurgy had long been carried on in parts of the area round the Mediterranean, they still depended on the use of flint and stone tools. The most important of these were the blades of axes and adzes, which were mounted on wooden handles and used for clearing forests, shaping timbers for houses and tombs, hollowing out boats, and roughing out all manner of small equipment like bowls and ladles. Tools of this family had indeed already been brought into use among Mesolithic hunter-fishers during the early forest period, but among the Neolithic peasants a smoother finish and a more effective edge was given by means of polishing and grinding; besides, greater trouble was taken to secure the most suitable materials even from distant sources. By the latter part of Neolithic times in Britain the trade in flint and stone axe- and adze-blades was organised on an elaborate basis. The most desirable flint was mined from the chalk of East Anglia, Sussex and Wessex, either from shallow bell-shaped pits or, where necessary, from deeper shafts with galleries radiating from their bottoms. Round the pit-heads the blades were roughed out from their parent nodules and then chipped neatly into shape ready for export. Equally, where particularly desirable stone—tough, yet easily flaked—outcropped, regular manufactories grew up for flaking axe- and adze-blades from the scree, as at Graig Lwyd on the slopes of Penmaenmawr in North Wales, or at Pike of Stickle, Langdale, in the Lake District. Finished products from these workshops have been traced far afield—Langdale stone, for instance, as far as Scotland, the Isle of Man, Yorkshire, the Cambridge Region, the Middle Thames, and in Wessex down to the coast of Dorset. The intricate pattern of trade routes, revealed by a study of the distribution of the products of these and other axe factories, shows that the various parts of Britain were far more closely knit together at this time than had recently been thought. Moreover, both mines and factories imply that specialists laboured through at least a large part of the year on their crafts, depending for their food and other wants on the returns of trade.

The spread of copper-mining and tin-washing in the barbarian world must have been inspired ultimately by the needs of higher cultures in and around the East Mediterranean, yet the existence of the axe trade makes it easier to understand how a native bronze industry, based on the combination of metals found in different parts of the country, could grow up during a few generations. The exact sources of the copper used in Bronze Age Britain have not yet been closely defined, but it is certain that they must have been somewhere in the highland zone. The same need to avoid the carriage of waste matter, which led to the working of axe-blades at the quarries of flint and stone, caused copper to be smelted close to the parent lodes. The distribution of moulds, on the other hand, shows that bronzes were moulded in areas devoid of copper lodes, and it may be assumed that metal was traded in the form of crude cakes, of scrap and probably also of ingots. Tin, however, most of which must have been washed from the Cornish stream-beds, could well have been traded as a concentrate in bags, as well as in the form of ingots.

The introduction of bronze for tools and weapons was, of course, a gradual affair. To begin with,

D

copper was employed alone, and even when a true native bronze industry had grown up, the new material was used only for quite a narrow range of products, notably daggers, rapiers, halberd-blades and spear-heads, and above all the axes needed for felling and working timber. Flint and stone continued to be extensively used until metal became cheap enough during the Late Bronze Age to be made into such tools as knives, carpenter's chisels and gouges, and also metal-smith's anvils.

When iron was first introduced into Britain around the middle of the first millennium B.C. it was employed to copy forms previously made in bronze, and it was only when the smiths discovered the peculiar pro-perties of the new metal that they began to turn out the new types which ultimately shaped the material basis of the modern world. (Among the new tools and appliances made of cheap wrought iron may be noted farming equipment like ploughshares, coulters, digging-tools, scythes and bill-hooks, as well as craftsman's kit like frame-saws, hinged tongs, shears and iron-bladed rotary lathes.) Although iron ore was much more widely distributed in nature than those of copper or tin, certain ores were preferred, and the distribution of sword-moods in southern Britain suggests that the Forest of Dean was already a main source in pre-Roman times.

Many of the crafts most important in the life of prehistoric Britain have perished, leaving small trace behind them. Enough woodwork remains, though, to illustrate the influence of changes in the basic materials of tools. Thus in Neolithic times wooden containers had to be hollowed laboriously out of single blocks, but by the Late Bronze Age it was possible to make large, comparatively thin-walled buckets with separate bases sprung into grooves. Again, the introduction of the iron-bladed rotary lathe in La Tène times meant that all manner of vessels, as well as such things as wheel-hubs and spokes, could be turned with ease and grace. Some of the basic crafts, like leather-working—fine-eyed needles used for this came from Kent's Cavern and from Church Hole, Creswell—and also netting and plaiting, were inherited from the old hunting and gathering economy. Others, like potting and weaving, were introduced by farmers. The former may have attracted undue attention owing to the permanency of its products and their value to the archæologist for establishing sequences and identifying cultural traditions, yet it was undoubtedly an important craft in many, though not all, peasant communities. The great bulk of prehistoric pottery was made by hand for home use; it was not until a late stage of the Early Iron Age that it was made on the wheel. Although weaving was carried on with skill among Neolithic peasants on the continent, there is no certain evidence for its practice in Britain until the Bronze Age. Even from this period only impressions and scraps have generally survived, and these due in the main to the practices of putting cremated remains in textile bags and wrapping bronzes intended for the dead in pieces of cloth. Sheep wool was most commonly used for textiles though latterly horsehair was also employed (see Plate 9). The importance of weaving during the Early Iron Age is testified by the common occurrence of weaving-combs, spindle-whorls and loom-weights, and by the occasional presence of parts of the looms themselves. Textiles were of course used for clothing and also for wall-hangings, and in this connection the importance of dyestuffs must not be forgotten.

Over and above what was made at home or in different parts of Britain, our prehistoric forebears obtained certain things from overseas in return for native products. It is exciting to find, in the rich tombs of the Wessex Bronze Age, not only beads of amber, probably imported from the coast of Jutland by way of Germany, but also faience beads of Egyptian manufacture and goldsmith's work, betraying the influence of distant Mycenæ. Again, the Greek appetite for tin brought some things from the Mediterranean to Cornwall, though in this trade the middlemen seem to have taken the main profit. When the Romans conquered Gaul, Britain was brought even more definitely within the commercial orbit of the civilised world. Nothing emphasises more clearly the economic subservience of the barbarians than the lists of exports and imports set out by Strabo. The Britons yielded primary products like corn, cattle, hides, metals, hunting-dogs and slaves: in return they got such things as 'ivory bracelets and necklaces, amber, vessels of glass and small wares', though the wine, which archæology allows us to add, does something to balance the account.

The idea of minting coins was first introduced by Belgic immigrants; it is instructive to note that the earliest British coins, dating from towards the middle of the first century B.C., were ultimately inspired by Greece. It appears that gold staters of Philip II of Macedon, taken as loot from the Macedonian or Syrian wars to Rome, were introduced to Gaul and there served as models for the first native coinage from which our own was derived. All trade transactions in earlier times must presumably have been carried on by barter, or in terms of some primitive currency like ingots or cattle.

Since the ocean waters, fed by the melting ice-sheets, flooded over the North Sea bed and finally insulated Britain, trade and immigrants from the continent have had to cross the open sea. Dug-out canoes hollowed out from single tree-trunks have been found commonly enough, but such were used for traffic on inland waterways, the servicing of crannogs, lake-villages and

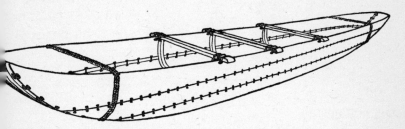

Fig. ii.   Prehistoric sewn wooden boat from North Ferriby,
Yorkshire, over fifty feet in length.

the like. The earliest sea-going boats were probably made of hides drawn over light frames, like those which survive in modified form in the Irish curragh. Such boats were doubtless used by the Obanians for their hunting and fishing, as well as for crossing to the mainland from the islands on which many of them lived. Study of the Neolithic axe-trade has shown that sea-crossings between the mainland of Britain and Ireland, the Isle of Man, and even the Channel Islands and the Breton coast, must commonly have been made in the normal course of commerce, and the distribution of megalithic chamber-tombs argues for even more widespread use of the Atlantic seaways. The ships of

the megalith-builders, though, like much else of
import, glide past us in the darkness of the prehistoric
night. The excellence of the workmanship on the
carvel-built sewn boats from North Ferriby on the
Humber, mere river-ferries as these were, argues that

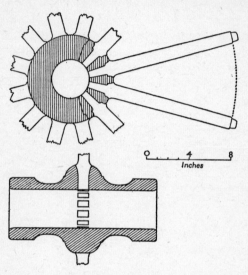

Fig. iii.   Wooden wheel-hub from the Glastonbury
lake-village.

British boat-building had already reached an extremely
high standard before the close of the prehistoric period.

By comparison, transport overland must always have
been arduous in early times. No evidence exists for
wheeled transport in Britain before the Late Bronze
Age. The chieftains of Iron Age Britain commanded
chariots for parade, rapid movement and war, but how
far wagons or carts were in workaday use is another
question. The unfinished wheels found at Glastonbury

may only show that village wheelwrights, whose virtuosity was quite astonishing, were turning out vehicles for their lords. Metalled roads, except for a few traces at centres like Camulodunum and Maiden Castle, did not exist in prehistoric Britain, but from the Late Bronze Age timber tracks began to be laid across bogs to carry cross-country routes to river-ferries, or give access to marsh settlements. However, the main lines of communication in prehistoric Britain continued to be waterways; it was from across the sea that traders and immigrants came to enrich and fertilise the life of the islanders.

SUGGESTIONS FOR FURTHER READING

V. Gordon Childe, *The Dawn of European Civilization*, 1925, 4th ed. enlarged and rewritten, 1947.

V. G. Childe, *Prehistoric Communities of the British Isles*, 1940, 3rd ed. 1949.

Grahame Clark, *Prehistoric England*, 1940, 4th ed. 1948.

Grahame Clark, *Prehistoric Europe: the Economic Basis*, 1951. (This book is especially relevant to the subject of the chapter.)

III

J. M. DE NAVARRO

The Celts in Britain and their Art

IN this chapter, as opposed to those which have preceded it, the theme narrows in scope, but in treatment it becomes more detailed.

What do we mean by the word Celts? Who were they? Where did they originate? When did they first reach these shores? A host of questions arises, and he would be a wise man who could answer them all, especially within the span of one short chapter.

The Celts lived at the source of the Danube, which rises in the Pyrenees. This is more or less what Herodotus writes, and it may serve as an example of the value of the earliest references to the Celts. While in Herodotus' time (the fifth century B.C.) Celts may well have inhabited the upper Danube basin, his location of the sources of that river seems to be somewhat vague! It is true that Hecatæus of Miletus locates the Greek colony of Massilia (Marseilles), traditionally founded *circa* 600 B.C., in *the territory of the Ligurians near the land of the Celts.* Hecatæus flourished about 500 B.C., and, from what he says, Celts by this time would seem to have been established in Gaul; in other words, before the La Tène period began.

Archæologists divide the Iron Age of a great part of temperate Europe into an earlier, Hallstatt, and a later, La Tène, period. The names are derived from two sites: Hallstatt in Austria and La Tène in Switzerland. They are convenient labels, little more. Moreover, we are accustomed to speak of the La Tène culture as Celtic. Indeed for the fourth century B.C. (when the La Tène period had entered upon the second of the four phases into which it is sometimes divided) our knowledge of the Celts from classical sources is fuller. We know something of their movements and the geographical positions occupied at that time by certain Celtic peoples on the continent, and in most of the areas concerned the La Tène culture is represented. It would be less easy to establish that in the earliest of the four La Tène phases (say during the latter part of the fifth century B.C.) Celtic was the language spoken by the people among whom the La Tène culture then arose; yet the balance of probability is rather in favour of than against such an assumption.

The term 'Celtic' has just been used in a linguistic sense. When the Celts first came into direct contact with the Romans and Greeks, classical authors refer to a tall, fair element among them. Actually the Celts by this time were too mixed for one to speak of a Celtic race; and if the term Celtic has any clear significance, it merely refers to peoples whose language was a Celtic one.

Celtic forms part of that large family of languages known as Aryan or Indo-European. The early home of Celtic probably lay in western Germany; and some would locate it in the south of that area, between the middle Rhine and the upper Danube basins. But Chadwick [1] has recently advanced strong arguments for a more northerly location: in the Lower Rhenish area and the region to the east and north-east of it. This view certainly fits in well with the evidence for Britain, as Britain was invaded on more than one occasion from that direction.

This leads to one of the most disputed subjects in early British antiquity: when did the Celts first set foot in this country? I can only touch upon this difficult problem here.

The two most popular archæological interpretations are that the Celts first reached Britain either in the Late Bronze Age, or, far earlier, in the Beaker stage. Both views are hard to establish.

The difficulty about the Late Bronze Age theory is perhaps mainly an archæological one. It is by no means agreed that the introduction of the Late Bronze Age civilisation into these islands—with its new economy (cheaper metal, and the reorganisation of the distributive side of the industry), its novel technical processes, together with its new types of weapons—was diffused by an invasion. Mahr [2] and Chadwick [3] believe that it was, and, what is more, that along with these changes the invaders introduced the Celtic language. It is true that there was a Late Bronze Age movement into this country from northern France, and the Netherlands, by a people known to archæologists as the Deverel-Rimbury folk. But even if they reached Britain at the outset of the Late Bronze Age (which some doubt), their characteristic pottery is, with rare exceptions, limited to the south of a line drawn from the Wash to the Bristol Channel, whereas the new types of weapon (socketed axes and slashing swords) are found over the greater part of the British Isles. The wider distribution of these types, and with them (as Mahr and Chadwick believe) the diffusion of the Celtic language, cannot be ascribed to a further large-scale expansion within these islands of the Deverel-Rimbury elements until evidence for such an expansion can be established. At present this is non-existent.

As for the Beaker theory, the difficulty is perhaps mainly linguistic. The Celtic languages in these islands fall into two groups: Q-Celtic, which is regarded as the earlier form (Irish, Gaelic, Manx), and P-Celtic (Welsh, Cornish); or, in the old but more familiar terminology of Sir John Rhŷs, Goidelic and Brythonic. The *qu*-sound is preserved in Q-Celtic, while in P-Celtic it becomes labialised: for example, the *maq* (*mac*) of Irish and Gaelic becomes *map* in Welsh. If the first Q-Celts reached this country in so remote a time as the Beaker stage, the differences between Q-Celtic and P-Celtic would surely be more fundamental than in fact they are: for on this reckoning no subsequent invasions which could have introduced P-Celtic took place before the Late Bronze or earliest Iron Age— roughly a thousand or more years later than the Beaker movements into this country.

Is it possible that the first Celts to reach Britain were Iron Age A elements? (See below, p. 62 ff.) Space does not permit a detailed discussion of what might be termed the fortieth article of an Irishman's faith—that no Q-Celt reached Ireland who had first set foot in Britain. The lack of Q-Celtic place-names in England is generally advanced in support of this view. All one can say of it is that, if it is true, Q-Celtic must first have been introduced into Ireland from the continent direct by stray bands of adventurers, who have left no trace in the archæological record. This is not inherently impossible. Such a view might even be advanced for the introduction of Celtic into Great Britain. All linguistic changes are not of necessity the result of invasion: the spread of the English language into the Scottish Highlands, for example, was not effected by a large scale, archæologically attestable movement of a people.

Even from what has been said, it will be evident to the reader how difficult it can be to equate a people speaking a given language with a given archæological culture—especially when dealing with times of which there were no written records.

Although classical authors do not actually describe the Britons as Celtic-speaking, the evidence of the names of certain British peoples, persons and places (especially names of natural features); to say nothing of the fundamental resemblance between the material cultures of these islands and those of the Celtic area upon the continent; the existence of a Druidic order on both sides of the English Channel: all go to show that by Roman times at least the greater part of Britain was Celtic-speaking. And perhaps we have a clue that this was not of recent date in Cæsar's statement that the interior (by which he means the non-Belgic parts of Britain) was inhabited by peoples declared in their own tradition to be indigenous to this island. (For the Belgæ see below, p. 66.) This suggests that, by the middle of the first century B.C., the Celtic movements into the non-Belgic parts of this country had been forgotten: for it is unthinkable that the first Celts to reach this island did not arrive until after Cæsar's departure in 54 B.C.

The claim here put before the reader is a less ambitious one and may well err on the conservative side: it is that, whenever the first Celts arrived in Britain, by the time this country had entered upon its La Tène period (probably in the third century B.C. and thus roughly two hundred years before Cæsar's expeditions) the population of Britain was mainly Celtic-speaking, and it is chiefly with the La Tène period that this chapter is concerned.

The La Tène period began upon the continent during the latter part of the fifth century B.C., and lasted in different regions till the Roman conquests or to a period when the influence of Roman civilisation became the dominant cultural factor. It covers therefore the greater part, though not the beginning, of the Celtic Migration Period—that phase of history when the Celts, attaining to their greatest expansion, occupied a not strictly continuous zone stretching from the Atlantic coasts into Asia Minor. Vast though it was, this expansion was an ephemeral one in its effects. To give but one example: the Celtic language has long died out upon the continent, apart from Brittany, where it was reintroduced by British refugees fleeing from the Anglo-Saxons; elsewhere it is only in these islands that Celtic languages survive to-day.

Upon the continent the La Tène period can be divided into four phases, which are known by the first four letters of the alphabet. The Early Iron Age in Britain, according to the now generally accepted system of Professor C. F. Hawkes, falls into three divisions known as Iron Age, A, B and C. The latter are more complex than they at first appear: they are capable of subdivision, they can overlap each other, and they are also capable of influencing and fusing with each other, thus, for example, giving rise to hybrid AB groups. In a rough and very simplified form the following table shows the correlations between the continental and British phases in question:

CONTINENTAL	BRITISH
End of Hallstatt La Tène A La Tène B	Iron Age A, surviving still later in places
End of La Tène B, La Tène C, and start of La Tène D	The earlier Iron Age B groups (pre-Belgic La Tène)
La Tène D and early Gallo-Roman	Later Iron Age B groups (non-Belgic La Tène) and Iron Age C (Belgic La Tène)

Note that hybrid British AB groups are met with, dating from La Tène C and later, some not uninfluenced by Iron Age C.

Roughly speaking, then, British Iron Age A corresponds with the end of Hallstatt (see below, p. 63) and with the continental La Tène Phases A and (most of) B, though in places it survived later still. The earlier (pre-Belgic) Iron Age B corresponds with the end of continental La Tène B, with all La Tène C and, in time, with the opening of continental La Tène D. British Iron Age C or Belgic La Tène may be correlated with the greater part of continental La Tène D and with what in Gaul are the beginnings of the Gallo-Roman period. It will be seen that British Iron Age C has an ethnic as well as a cultural and chronological significance, and that contemporary with it are later Iron Age B groups which may be described as non-Belgic, in contradistinction to the earlier British Iron Age B groups which I have termed pre-Belgic.

Iron Age A is Hallstatt in tradition, though, chronologically, the greater part of it falls within the span of

time when the La Tène period was running its course
upon the continent.   As I see it, the earliest of the Iron
Age A movements (which reached lowland Britain
from the Dutch and German Lower Rhenish areas) do
actually date from late Hallstatt times and perhaps
took place round about 500 B.C., though some would
place them slightly later.

Late in the fifth century or soon after (also in Iron
Age A) very late Hallstatt elements (named Jogassians
after the site of Les Jogasses, near Épernay) moved
into southern Britain from north-east Gaul.   From
that area they seem to have been ousted by a warlike
group of La Tène peoples, who were establishing
themselves in the Marne and the adjacent regions.   In
England, the pottery of this Jogassian element is
frequently coated with hæmatite, a red iron ore found
in northern France, but not in the area of the primary
diffusion of this pottery in England.   It consists of
sharp-angled bowls which are often associated with
shouldered pots;   the pots can also be coated with
hæmatite.   Both types are sometimes decorated, but
the decoration is simple: furrows, cordons or incised
motifs on the bowls;   stab and drag, finger-printing on
the pots.   Our knowledge of Iron Age A is mainly
based on settlement material, and the settlements
(whether open villages, lone steadings or hill-forts),
though often rich in pottery, yield few metal objects.
Late Bronze Age objects on the one hand, and La Tène
B types on the other, have come to light on sites dating
from Iron Age A, which maintained its Hallstatt
tradition deep into the La Tène period.   The culture
may be described as a peaceful, peasant culture.

During the earlier half of the third century B.C. there
was a movement into southern England from the Marne

and districts adjacent to it in France; it was the first of a series of Iron Age B movements into this country. It introduced a number of La Tène types: certain forms of pottery, brooches and horse-harness and even chariots. In form the chariot was a light two-wheeled vehicle, and at the back had a pair of projecting horns which could be grasped by the person jumping on to it; it was drawn by two horses. The chariot was still being used in warfare by the Britons in Cæsar's time, when, on the continent, it had given place to cavalry in fighting.

Iron Age B is definitely La Tène, both in time and in character. The advent of these martial Marnians is thought to have caused the Iron Age A population of southern England to fortify their steadings and to erect a whole series of hill-forts with single ramparts and simple entrance defences. But for all this the two elements merged, and in a number of districts hybrid AB groups were formed.

The Marnians spread north into Yorkshire—probably along a corridor of open country known as the Jurassic route—where the chariot-graves of the East Riding, with their uncremated bodies, are evidently the last resting-places of their ruling classes. The Greek geographer Ptolemy, who flourished in the second century A.D., speaks of a people in what is now east Yorkshire called the Parisii (the name is of course preserved in that of Paris in France). Thanks to the finding of an inscription, Petuaria, the chief town of these north British Parisii, is known during the first century A.D. to have been at Brough-on-Humber. So, strange as it may seem, there is a Parisian strain in the ancestry of the Yorkshireman.

About the time of this Marnian incursion into

England another movement reached Scotland from overseas, and probably from the same quarter. It introduced the La Tène culture into the more northern parts of Great Britain. The numerous vitrified forts of Scotland are now known to be *muri-gallici* (as Cæsar calls them), strongholds built of stone walls reinforced with timber, originally introduced by these newcomers, which, whether by accident or design, have undergone the action of fire. Chadwick very plausibly believed that these invaders introduced into Scotland a language closely akin to Welsh ('Welsh-Pictish' is his name for it), which has left its traces in a number of Scottish place-names (see his *Early Scotland*, Chapter IV).

The different Iron Age B movements and groups are very complex, and mention can only be made of some of them. Among pre-Belgic B elements is the Cornish group—with its cliff castles, stone ring-forts, courtyard houses, and its pottery stamped with duck motifs. It probably came from Brittany, perhaps toward the end of the second century B.C., doubtless attracted to Cornwall by its tin. Later this element spread into the Cotswolds, with its characteristic duck-stamped pottery, which in one instance had grit of Cornish granite in the paste.

The later (non-Belgic) Iron Age B groups, which were contemporary with Iron Age C (Belgic La Tène), were mainly due to later movements from northern France, especially Brittany. Among these emigrants were the builders of (or perhaps one should say the chiefs who caused to be built) the great multivallate hill-forts with complex entrances; in its developed form, Maiden Castle, Dorset, is a classic example.

Perhaps peoples from the same quarter reached the lake villages of Somerset at what was probably a late

E

date in the occupation of these sites. At all events, the decorated pottery found on them shows affinities with certain decorated La Tène vessels from Brittany, although elaborations of the ornament (wave patterns and trumpet scrolls) took place in this country. The decorated pottery of these Somerset settlements is limited to their latest levels, a fact not always realised. This is one of the most interesting of the British Iron Age groups; for the finds from these sites give a more detailed picture of the way in which people lived at that time than do those from most of the other groups under discussion. Some mention of this aspect of the settlements will be found in Chapter II.

Iron Age C (as opposed to Iron Age B) is Belgic La Tène. The Belgæ, who were of mixed Celto-Teutonic ancestry, are thought to have reached south-east Britain at about 75 B.C. from the area to the south of the Ardennes. Cæsar says that their language differed from the Celts'; but according to Strabo the differences seem to have been merely of dialect. From south-east England the newcomers expanded into coastal Essex and Hertfordshire, and a little later into the Cambridge region. They spread westward, too, into Wessex. This expansion caused further movements and unrest among the neighbouring non-Belgic peoples: the terrible massacre, evidences of which were found in the main entrance of the hill-fort on Bredon, Gloucestershire, may perhaps be connected with such repercussions. The defenders were literally cut to pieces, their limbs and trunks pitched pell-mell to one or other side of the entrance; their heads were apparently impaled on the gate which was then set on fire: charred fragments of skull were found below it. The rest of the bodies were left to rot where they lay.

Despite such occurrences, the Belgic settlement tended to have a centralising effect—the numerous smaller settlements, descendants of the earlier elements, tending to coalesce into fewer, larger ones. The Belgæ played a part in the development of urban life— witness such Belgic towns as Colchester and Præwood near Verulamium—perhaps in that of agriculture and certainly in the history of British coinage, a subject already referred to in the previous chapter. It was perhaps in this phase that the descent from the lighter-soiled hills began: for the Belgæ were a valley-dwelling people and appear to have used a heavier plough, capable of cultivating the heavier, fatter, low-lying areas. It was they, too, who introduced pottery turned upon the fast wheel.

Shortly before the advent of the Romans, the Catu-vellaunian dynasty, with its capital now at Colchester, had, under its great king Cunobelin (the Cymbeline of Shakespeare), gained political control over a large part of southern England, and, in fostering ever closer relations with Rome, done much toward paving the way for the Romanisation of the country.

The evidence of classical authors, such as that of Cæsar and Tacitus, throws further light on conditions in Britain during the first century B.C. and the first century of our era; it is especially valuable for the information it gives about the less tangible aspects of civilisation—government, religion and the like.

While in Gaul of Cæsar's time, apart from the Belgic area in the north-east, we meet with a definitely republican constitution—in Britain kingship seems to have been universal. Moreover, we learn from Tacitus and others of such women-rulers as Boudicca (Boadicea) and the slippery Cartimandua, queens of the Iceni in East Anglia and the Brigantes in the north of England.

Both Cæsar and Tacitus speak of Druids in this country; and Cæsar even writes that the druidic rule of life was discovered in Britain, and how those who wished to study it more closely came to this country to do so. It is possible that Stonehenge, at a very advanced date in its long history, may have been the scene of druidic rites. Further evidence, though of more recent date, that throws light upon religion, is afforded by inscriptions on Romano-British altars.

Amid this welter of As, Bs and Cs, to say nothing of Ps and Qs, the reader may well ask what the people themselves were really like. It is true that Cæsar and others give a certain amount of information about the Britons. But for a full-length portrait of a Celt one must turn to the pages of Diodorus Siculus, who flourished in the latter half of the first century B.C. but evidently drew his information from an earlier source, thought to be the lost work of Posidonius the Stoic, which described his travels in Gaul about 100 B.C. Diodorus writes:

The Gauls are tall of stature and fair in complexion. Not only is their hair bright by nature, but they do their best to increase this natural peculiarity of its colour by preparations: for they are ever smearing the hair with a thick wash of chalk and drawing it back from the brow to the crown and to the nape of the neck, so that their appearance resembles that of hob-goblins and pucks—for their hair is so weighted down and stiffened by the preparation, that it is just like the mane of a horse.

Some shave their chins, while others grow short beards. But the nobles have their cheeks shaven and let their moustaches grow so long that their mouths are covered up; and so when they eat, these get entangled in the food, while their drink is taken in, as it were, through a strainer. . . .

They wear amazing clothes: shirts, with flowing patterns and dyed all kinds of colours, and trousers called *brakai* (breeches); and they wear cloaks, fastened over their shoulders with a brooch, . . . divided all over by squares, decorated with flowers.

Their appearance is remarkable and their voices deep-sounding and exceedingly harsh. In conversation they are sparing of words and enigmatical, and generally they express only half of what they mean. They deal much in exaggeration in their talk, with a view to magnifying themselves and belittling others. They are boastful by nature; but their intellects are keen and they are not slow to acquire knowledge. . . .

When they have slain their enemies, they cut off their heads. . . . They nail these trophies up on the walls of their houses, just as hunters do with wild beasts which they have slain. But the heads of their most distinguished enemies they preserve carefully and keep in a box and show to their visitors, glorying in the fact that they, or one of their ancestors, have been offered a large sum for such and such a head, and have refused the offer, . . . in which they display a kind of barbaric *noblesse*.

Of their women, Ammianus Marcellinus writes in the fourth century A.D.: 'A whole band of foreigners would be unable to cope with a single Gaul, if he called his wife to his aid, who is usually very strong and with blue eyes; especially when swelling her neck, gnashing her teeth and brandishing her sallow arms of huge proportions, she begins to strike blows mingled with kicks, as if they had been so many bolts sent from the string of a catapult.' On the strength of this passage, one is tempted to argue an early origin for French boxing!

If one may generalise, the picture which classical authors give points, on the whole, to conditions in Britain being somewhat more backward than in Gaul— perhaps a generation or so behind the times—in all but one thing, in art. Even this unfolded later here than abroad; but at its best it was unsurpassèd, and in independence and imaginative power unexcelled by the finest La Tène masterpieces which the continent has to show.

In order to place the La Tène art of these islands in its proper perspective, a brief description of the genesis and development of the style upon the continent is necessary—a theme fruitful in more ways than one: for an examination, however brief, of the problem throws considerable light on the genesis and the starting-point of the La Tène culture as a whole.

On the continent, as we saw, the La Tène period can be divided into four phases. During the first three of these, Paul Jacobsthal, our leading authority, the author of the monumental work, *Early Celtic Art*,[4] distinguishes three distinct and widespread styles upon the continent. Roughly and briefly stated, the phases and styles in question may be correlated as follows. Styles I and II correspond with Phases A and B, although Style II lasted long enough to overlap somewhat with Style III, which was in fashion during Phase C. This is shown by associated finds; and the two styles can even occur on the same object (see below, pp. 73–4).

Phase Style I (and with it Phase A) began during the later half of the fifth century B.C. There are two remarkable facts to remember about it: the sudden manner in which it unfolded, and its essentially aristocratic character. There are no groping steps toward perfection; it opened perfect, mature, overnight as it were. As Jacobsthal observes (on p. 162), 'it is the age of intensest foreign contacts, of ready reception'.[4] The sudden manner in which it appears is perhaps best explained by the importation of foreign artists from the south (mainly from Italy, to a far less extent from Greece) and perhaps from the east (South Russia, the Caucasus, Persia, Syria). In Style I there are actually three main components: the *classical*, seen for the most part, but not entirely, in plant motifs (palmettes, lotuses and the like), ultimately Greek, but with very rare exceptions derived through Italy (see Plate 11*b*); the *oriental* influences consisting of strange, unnaturally treated beast motifs and wild, nightmare masks (see Plate 11*a*); while the third component consists for the greater part of geometric patterns, to which should be added the duck motif (see Plate 10). The third (largely geometric) component I regard as partly a Hallstatt legacy, though earlier (ultimately Greek) tradition of the Southern Oriental-ising Styles is detectable. We speak of 'oriental influences' and use the word 'influence' because (with one possible exception) there are no eastern imports in the area of La Tène A, only ornament inspired from the east. If, as I believe, there were eastern artists at work for the Early La Tène chiefs, they did not contribute purely eastern models, but motifs, oriental in spirit, suited to the taste of their new patrons. The achievement of the creators of Style I was the welding together of these three disparate components into a unitary style, highly abstract in character, into what indeed may with some justice be claimed as one of the outstanding abstract arts of the world.

As to its aristocratic character, Style I only appears upon luxury articles, found, for the greater part, in princely graves—objects of adornment, weapons, table service, horse and chariot trappings.

This leads to the problem of where the La Tène culture first unfolded. Though centres of it are known in north-east France and in the Bohemian-Bavarian-West Austrian region, Style I is more richly represented in the Middle Rhenish zone than elsewhere; and if the genesis of that style is to be located in a single restricted area, it is that region which has the best claim to being its starting-point. Style I workshops have been identified there, and Jacobsthal thinks that there may have been a factory for chariots in that area. It may be that similar early workshops will be identified elsewhere, yet the artists who created Style I would naturally settle in the district where existed the greatest demand for their work, and this, as I have said, is most richly represented in the region just mentioned. Moreover, one can say with some assurance that their patrons were the wealthy princelings, men and women, who lie buried beneath a celebrated group of barrows known as the Middle Rhenish Chieftains' Graves. Most of these date from La Tène A, and are lavishly furnished, not only with southern imports (metal table-services from Italy and Greek pottery) and objects made of gold, but with many of the outstanding masterpieces of our Style I.

In Jacobsthal's second style, the oriental elements recede and the classical become dominant. The chief new feature derived from the south is the tendril: tendril motifs of different types, which are treated by

what are now *native* artists with a considerable degree
of independence. Style II corresponds roughly with
Phase B, and some of its leading masterpieces have
been dated to the outgoing decades of the fourth
century B.C. When it began is less certain; Jacobsthal
hazards about the middle of that century; if he is
right in placing it as late as this, we have no graves as
yet of the Celtic invaders of Italy, for Italy was invaded
by the Celts at about 400 B.C., and Style I (which on
Jacobsthal's dating must have still been current at
that date) is virtually unknown among the La Tène
finds made in that country.

Style II is more densely spread over a wider area
than the Early Style. Moreover, the objects embellished by its artists are no longer exclusively found
in graves of the ruling classes. Both the supply and
the demand were greater than in La Tène A, and
perhaps there is some connection between this and the
fact that in La Tène B southern imports to the north
of the Alps shrink in numbers almost to a vanishing-
point: the Celts had come to prefer their own work,
and this was now easier to obtain. Style II is the
earliest La Tène style to reach Britain, but it is very
sparsely represented here; an excellent example is
the horn-cap for a chariot found in the Thames at
Brentford (see fig. iv): the first British style was yet
to come. The ornament on the horn-cap from Brentford is a good instance of La Tène tendril design and
probably came from the Middle Rhenish area.

The overlap between Styles II and III is not only
shown by associated finds: we have actual instances
of the two styles appearing on the same object. The
scabbard from the Marne region (see Plate 13*a*) is an
instance of this: as Jacobsthal observes, the staple

medallions are embellished in Style II, while the main design on the actual sheath is an interesting example of the so-called sword substyle of Style III.

This leads on to the third style. The sheath just mentioned is one of the very rare examples of that style found in France; for the chief centres of the new school

Fig. iv. Bronze horn-cap from Brentford with ornament
of Style II. An import from the Rhenish area.

were now in Hungary and Switzerland. This style Jacobsthal divides into the sword (see Plate 13*b*) and the plastic substyles, both of which occur on objects assigned to La Tène C. In the latter the Celtic love of the weird, the uncanny, can be translated into purely abstract form (see Plate 12*a*). It was already used soon after the middle of the first half of the third century B.C., when classical authorities tell us, Celts had reached Thrace: for La Tène objects so embellished appear in a grave, evidently of that date, at Mezek, now in Bulgaria, then in Thrace.

Elements of Style III are almost, but not quite, unknown in Britain, but this style is none the less highly important for the British Isles, for out of it was evolved the first La Tène art of these islands, termed by Jacobsthal Style IV. Style IV appeared almost as suddenly and quite as fully formed as did Style I upon the continent, and, like it, is probably due to the bringing in of foreign artists, but this time from Hungary and Switzerland. Also, like Style I, it is purely aristocratic in character. One look at the objects it adorns shows this fact. Such an art could not have arisen 'in the glories of a classless paradise'. Its creators were obviously working for rich patrons, whether princely or priestly. You may ask, 'Why priestly?' Because out of hardly a dozen known works of this style, at least eight have been dredged up from rivers. Like the great La Tène find, discovered during the war on the now dried-up margin of a lake, Llyn Cerrig Bach, in Anglesey, they bear out the testimony of classical authors of the existence of the Celtic water cult.

In Style IV the motifs are both linear and plastic, the plastic being often adorned by the linear—the ornamenting of ornament is an unclassical feature. Palmettes, tendrils or scrolls are prominent, and the tendrils sprout into the most unnatural yet delightful leaves, which are often double contoured. Sometimes the tendrils have abstract bird-headed finials, as in the Style III design on the scabbard found in France (see Plate 13a). Animal heads added to non-animal ornament may, in the last resort, go back to Style I, in which they are one of the elements derived from the orient. The design sometimes moves to a circular rhythm. All these features are to be seen on the round shield-boss found in the Thames off Wandsworth (see fig. v).

Fig. v. Bronze circular shield boss from the Thames at
Wandsworth. A master-piece of Style IV.

But in other examples (sometimes due to the shape of the space to be filled) the design can move in other manners: compare the sword-locket found in the River Witham with the Style III scabbard from Hungary (see Plates 14, 13*b*). Another famous example is the shield, also found in the River Witham, once embellished with the charge of a boar, now only traceable by discoloration and the position of the rivet-holds which held it in position.

The Irish examples of this style were all found in Ulster and were probably imported from British workshops: a superb horse's frontlet of bronze from Torrs in south-west Scotland, which once adorned the study of Sir Walter Scott, suggests the route by which they came.

However, it has been pointed out that there were also La Tène artists actually at work in Ireland, though later, probably in the first century B.C. In a far earlier passage-grave at Lough Crew an artist or a colony of such artists had squatted, leaving there a number of bone trial pieces which bore La Tène ornament—a somewhat gloomy workshop! One of them, with a design related to the ornament on the gold torc from Broighter, Co. Londonderry, is shown together with the latter on p. 78 (figs. vi and vii). Three works of the same school have come to light in England and one in Scotland. Four out of this group of five objects, supposed to have come from one workshop, were of gold, and, as early as the Bronze Age, Ireland was the El Dorado of western Europe. The magnificent gold torc from Ken Hill, Snettisham, Norfolk, published in the *Illustrated London News*, 10th March, 1951, is either a work of this school, or is definitely influenced by it.

Among the most striking of the later varieties of

Fig. vi. Bone slip from Lough Crew, County Meath, with ornament akin to that in fig. vii.

Fig. vii. Detail of ornament on a gold torc from Broighter, County Londonderry.

British art was the so-called 'Mirror Style', which, though used to decorate the backs of bronze mirrors, appears upon other objects as well. Famous and frequently illustrated examples are the mirrors from Birdlip, Gloucestershire, and Desborough, Northamptonshire. What is probably an early example of this style occurs on a mirror in the Mayer collection, now in Liverpool Museum (see Plate 15*a*). Notice the combination of plain burnished with matted or basketry patterns and the inset circlets. Sir Cyril Fox, who has devoted much attention to this school of art, believes that it was originally a translation into two-dimensional form of such raised circles and domed trumpets as appear on a crescent plaque of bronze found at Llyn Cerrig (see Plate 15*b*), and he would date the genesis of this style at about 75–50 B.C. On the mirrors the whole ornamental field can be covered with primary and secondary motifs. The background thus has a life of its own. It is perhaps in the Mirror Style that the La Tène art of these islands attains its peak of abstraction: the rhythm of the designs harks back to that of earlier plant patterns; but the features used in ornament are really geometric—some of them borrowed from Rome. This style lasted into the first century A.D.

In La Tène D period we have also to reckon with the contribution of the Belgæ. But here only one or two features can be touched upon. It was the Belgæ who gave the real impetus to enamel work by using what is known as the champlevé technique to cover larger ornamental fields; hitherto it had been used more restrictedly. The terret from Bapchild, Kent (see Plate 16*c*) is an instance. Some enamel designs are akin to the Mirror Style. The innovation was taken over by enamellers in the non-Belgic area. There is in this country a series of hoards of such enamels; they date on the whole from round about the time the Romans landed. Among them is the hoard from Stanwick, Yorkshire, which contained a fine example of the Celtic love of what has been called the animalisation of ornament: a horse's head is suggested by two opposed trumpet-scrolls (see fig. viii). This treatment of ornament, as noted above (see p. 75), is already met with in Style I; it is one of that style's oriental components. Here we have something analogous cropping up later.

Fig. viii. Bronze plaque from Stanwick, Yorkshire.

There is literary evidence for British enamels: Philostratus, a sophist at the court of the emperor Severus' wife, writes: 'They say that the barbarians who live in the Ocean pour [these] colours on to heated bronze and that they adhere, and grow hard as stone, keeping the designs that are made in them.' At first red only was used; later other colours were added, giving a spotty, less pleasing effect.

More revolutionary still was the introduction by the Belgæ of naturalistic figures into these highly abstract surroundings. The bronze handle-escutcheon—a cow licking its muzzle—recently found with Belgic pottery at Felmersham, Beds., will serve as an example (see Plate 16*b*).

Finally, there are two famous pieces that I am not illustrating, as they have been so frequently reproduced: the Battersea shield [5] and the Aesica brooch. [6] A feature of the ornament of the shield has been compared with a similar feature found on Roman silver-work of the time of Augustus, and thus dates the shield at roughly about the time of our Lord's birth. The gilt brooch from Aesica is a rather elaborate form of the so-called 'thistle brooch'; it is now thought to have been made in the north of England about the time of Agricola's northern expedition in A.D. 80. It has been praised as one of the finest examples of British La Tène art. Actually, compared with some of the works illustrated in this chapter, it is rather flamboyant, not to say vulgar.

It is amazing to think how these artists, living amid the squalor, stink and barbarism of Iron Age surroundings (at Salmonsbury in Gloucestershire there is evidence which strongly suggests that shortly before the arrival of the Romans they were eating the marrow from the bones of their women), could attain the highly sophisticated simplicity of such works as the tankard handle from Trawsfynydd (see Plate 12*b*), or could achieve the dignity and repose of the bronze bowl from Ireland illustrated in Plate 16*a*.

By the time the legions landed this art was already enjoying its Indian summer. Nor did the Romans succeed in effacing the old traditions, either here or upon the continent. On the contrary, as Jacobsthal has observed when estimating the contribution of La Tène to the history of art: 'The classical forms and technical advances disseminated by the Celts over Europe prepared the soil for the following phase when the Celts, this time on a larger scale and with the Romans as powerful agents, dominated the minor arts of the Roman provinces.'[4]

NOTES

1. *The Nationalities of Europe*, pp. 150 ff., by H. M. Chadwick.

2. *Proceedings of the Prehistoric Society*, 1937, pp. 389 ff.

3. *Op. cit.*, p. 150; and Chadwick's *Early Scotland*, p. 79.

4. *Early Celtic Art*, by Paul Jacobsthal, was published in 1944 by the Clarendon Press; it is the classic treatment of the subject.

5. See *Guide to the British Museum Iron Age Antiquities*, frontispiece.

6. Leeds, *Celtic Ornament*, fig. 23c.

SUGGESTIONS FOR FURTHER READING

Apart from Jacobsthal's *Early Celtic Art* (1944), which is a work written for the specialist, the reader will find many illustrations of La Tène art in E. T. Leeds, *Celtic Ornament* (1933), and in the British Museum *Guide to Antiquities of the Early Iron Age* (1925). Jacobsthal's 'Imagery in Early Celtic Art' (*Proceedings of the British Academy*, xxvii) and 'Early Celtic Art,' a short paper by him in *The Burlington Magazine* for September 1935, are also recommended.

For a more general treatment of the Early Iron Age in Britain the reader is recommended to the relevant parts of Grahame Clark, *Prehistoric England* (1948); V. G. Childe, *Prehistoric Communities of the British Isles* (1949); J. and C. F. C. Hawkes, *Prehistoric Britain* (1947); Stuart Piggott, *British Prehistory* (Home University Library, 1949); T. D. Kendrick and C. F. C. Hawkes, *Archæology in England and Wales, 1914–1931* (1932).

IV

MARTIN CHARLESWORTH

The Roman Occupation

PREVIOUS chapters have demonstrated how the island of Britain was first peopled and settled, and narrated the stages through which its tribes progressed—some more rapidly than others—towards a fully agricultural civilisation. By the third century B.C. a fair portion of our island had been occupied by or come under the dominance of immigrant Celts. Their astonishing artistic faculty has been already described in Chapter III; descendants of the Celtic languages are still spoken in the western and northern parts of the island; many of the names they gave to our rivers and mountains (*e.g.* Avon, Dee, Derwent, Esk; Brent, Malvern, Penyghent) have survived in use in England proper till to-day. In the south-east there had been migrations of the Belgæ (p. 66), the last wave of which in about 75 B.C. (the Iron Age C folk) brought a new and deeper-going type of plough, which attacked and brought under cultivation the heavier soils. These Belgæ had introduced some sort of tribal organisation under a king, with a currency in gold and silver and a capital in eastern Essex. But save for this south-eastern region the country as a whole was disunited, inhabited by tribes ranging widely in the scale of organisation and culture. In the first half of the first century, however, this island was suddenly called upon to confront a world Power far more mature in its civilisation, and incomparably better organised whether for war or peace—the Roman Empire. The Romans were to overrun and occupy a large part of our island, to mould and change the face of the land, so to govern, defend and civilise it that, when their forces finally departed in the early fifth century, the inhabitants were for many years still proud to consider themselves *Romani* and to call Latin 'our language'. That occupation lasted from A.D. 43 to about 410—a space of some three hundred and sixty-seven years, or roughly as long a period as from the defeat of the Spanish Armada to the present day. A great deal may happen in three hundred and sixty-seven years, and the aim of this chapter is to investigate not so much what the Romans did, as to whether they left any permanent impress upon this country. In other words, the historian must try to answer three questions: Was the occupation an episode merely? Did the Romans depart leaving not a trace behind? Was there any 'legacy' from that occupation? In the opinion of the present writer there was a legacy, and a considerable one, but before detailing it a brief glance at the history of the island under the Romans is necessary, if for no other reason than because wars and fighting left considerable monuments behind.

It may be asked why there should have been an occupation at all. Indeed that question is salutary, because we are so accustomed to the fact that the Romans were here, it is so much a part of our general knowledge, that we are apt to regard it as almost in the order of things. But it was not. It is true that Julius Cæsar, when conquering France, had found it necessary to make two demonstrations in Britain, in 55 and 54 B.C., and had imposed a tribute upon the conquered Britons. But that tribute had lapsed, and though an independent Britain could be represented as a dangerous neighbour for a conquered Gaul, and though it offered a target for an ambitious emperor, no steps were taken to reconquer the island for practically a hundred years. Augustus had more important problems to cope with, and it was plausibly argued that tribute from our island would not repay the cost of an occupying garrison. But Claudius, who became emperor in 41, had a special motive: he needed a great military exploit, which would keep his armies busy, to inaugurate his reign, and it may also be that an erroneous notion of geography, which placed Ireland in a midway position between north-western Spain and south-western England, gave rise to a grandiose scheme for incorporating that island too in the Empire.

So in 43 after careful planning the great expedition started. It was a formidable task; four legions and a corresponding number of auxiliary troops were to be used, and an experienced commander was chosen, Aulus Plautius. The whole force must have been well over forty thousand men. Claudius himself crossed to Britain, to witness the final battle and the capture of Camulodunum (Colchester), and after, presumably, giving instructions for the organisation of the new province and for further advances, left after sixteen days' stay. There followed a rapid progress over the lowland country; already, by the year 50, the Rivers Severn and Trent marked the civil boundary; twenty-five years later, in spite of a violent revolt in East Anglia which resulted in more conciliatory measures towards the conquered population, the limits could be indicated roughly by a line on the map joining the towns of Exeter, Caerleon, Wroxeter, Chester and York. Already, too, though Colchester was intended to be the capital of the province, London was rapidly rising to eminence as a commercial centre, and the road system of the province radiated from it as a hub.

In or about 77 a new governor arrived, Gnaeus Julius Agricola. He must have known Britain and its problems well, for he had already served there twice, first on the governor's staff, and again in command of the XXth Legion; and he was a man of considerable military and administrative ability. In seven years' rapid campaigning he seems to have reached a point well north of Aberdeen, and even possibly as far as Inverness, from which he dispatched his fleet to circumnavigate the rest of the island. Thus when he retired he left a vastly enlarged province. It included all the north of England; along the 'isthmus' from Tyne to Eden ran a line of forts, and a road connecting them (the later *Stanegate*), while to the south trunk and lateral roads were completed or under construction. It included, too, all the Southern Uplands of Scotland (save for Galloway), while a second line of forts guarded the isthmus between Forth and Clyde, and here two trunk roads and two lateral roads were under construction. Even farther north the country may have been occupied for a time, though probably about the year 100 reasons of state compelled the retirement of Roman forces from Scotland to the more southerly line of forts between Corbridge and Carlisle.

About a generation later, when a new system of defence of the frontiers by continuous artificial barriers had been developed, great projects were begun in

Britain. In the year 123, by direction of the emperor Hadrian, the English Roman Wall was begun. This was built in stone (though for purposes of speed the westerly section had first to be completed in turf) over a distance of about 73 miles, along a line corresponding to the modern route from Newcastle by Corbridge and Greenhead to Carlisle, and ending at Bowness, where the Solway ceases to be fordable at low water. It was to be a patrolled barrier: in front lay a formidable ditch, then came the Wall itself, normally 8 feet broad and 15 feet high, with a patrol track on top; with ramparts and merlons it must have been about 20 feet high, and could effectively hold up raiding parties. In A.D. 142 came an advance, and a new frontier, which we may call the Scottish or Caledonian Roman Wall, was established. It was built not in stone but in turf, and extended for about 37 miles, from Carriden on the east to Old Kilpatrick on the west. Turf is both easier to handle and more economical; we may trace here the first recorded instance of Caledonian influence on British history. So for fifty years, roughly from 140 to 190, the Southern Uplands became effectively a part of the Roman Empire.

But now a civil war broke out in the Empire itself, and one ambitious claimant for the throne, Clodius Albinus, crossed the Channel to fight for his claim. By so doing he denuded the island of troops, and disaster followed, with barbarians flooding over the northern half of the province, wrecking, destroying and looting. Not until 210 was the emperor Septimius Severus able seriously to deal with the tasks of punishing the barbarians and of restoration. The English Wall was repaired and brought back into use (it had been dismantled while the Scottish Wall was guarded).

To the north of it certain outlying posts, at High Rochester, Risingham, Netherby and Birrens, were repaired, and occupied by bodies of scout troops. Henceforward the frontier corresponded more or less to the line of the present border between England and Scotland; to the north of it lay tribes that were being steadily won over to friendly relations, the Votadini and the Damnonii. (See Plate 17.)

So successful were these measures of Severus that for a considerable part of the third century, though much of the Empire was being harried by invaders, our country enjoyed peace and a real measure of prosperity. But towards the close of it threats from new regions, from Saxons on the east and Irish on the west, demanded a new system of defences. In East Anglia and the south-eastern counties a chain of forts was erected, stretching from Brancaster (near the Wash) by Dover and Pevensey to the Isle of Wight. Each fort was usually sited on a river or by a harbour, so that a flotilla attached to it could give early warning of the approach of raiders, while the cavalry garrison could deal with attempted landings. On the west traces are not so clear or consistent: signal-stations on the North Devon coast (Old Burrow and Martinhoe, near Lynton), late forts at Caer Seiont (Caernarvon) and Caer Gybi (Holyhead), suggest an elaborate scheme of coastal watching and defences, which may even have extended up to the Cumbrian coast, but the evidence is not yet sufficient for any scholar to pronounce definitely.

Still, these defence measures, whoever initiated and developed them (for there are signs of later remodelling), seem to have been extremely successful for at least two generations. But now came something hitherto unprecedented: the barbarians, baffled in separate attacks, combined together in a concerted onslaught, and swept in simultaneous invasion over the whole country. The ensuing devastation and destruction were frightful; it was a mortal blow to the prosperity of the island, and from now on deterioration set in. But this barbarian pressure had been increasing steadily all over the Empire; forces must be withdrawn somewhere to protect the core of the Empire, and so it seemed safer to evacuate the Wall, about 383, since the neighbouring and now allied Votadini and Damnonii could be trusted to guard that region. But less than thirty years later the whole situation of the Empire looked so precarious that the emperor Honorius determined to summon back all the Roman armed forces from the island, and told the British cities they must 'look after themselves'. Whether he meant this as a temporary expedient, or as permanent policy, cannot be ascertained; whatever he may have hoped, the situation steadily worsened, and about 418 came a final evacuation of all civilian staff and records. So ended the Roman occupation of Britain.

It may seem reasonable at this point to pause and inquire why the Romans retained their grip on this island for so long; there certainly had been moments when it might have been abandoned without severe loss of prestige, and the Romans were too practical to hold on to a losing proposition. It was certainly a good training-ground for armies, and the forces garrisoned here could be kept in fighting trim, and if necessary could be shipped swiftly across to France or Germany, as, for example, the IInd Augustan Legion was transferred to the continent about 275. Secondly, during the late second to the early fourth century its economic wealth was considerable; mines were in active production and crops abundant. Britain was a land of big country estates (*villæ*) and their associated rural industries, and it possessed a supply of skilled craftsmen, at a time when other provinces had been damaged by barbarian inroads. Probably it took fully a hundred years from the conquest before the exploitation of Britain's resources became profitable, but after that it must have merited the description of 'a very wealthy island' which one later writer applies to it.

Still, though the occupation may have been profitable, in the end it terminated: the Romans did withdraw. The main question still awaits an answer. Was there any 'legacy'? If so, of what nature was it? What was the enduring impression? After all, this country is not governed by a senate; its inhabitants do not speak a Romance language; our law system is not based upon the Roman. At first sight it might seem as though, apart from the imposing remains of walls, forts and camps, and the tracks of roads, nothing has survived. Yet some facts stand out.

First, it may be claimed that the notion of Britain as a unity, one country under one ruler, first emerged clearly under the Romans, and this notion endured in later tradition. The governor was the Count of Britain; later British kings claimed the title of *Prydein Wledig* (Lord of Britain). The Anglo-Saxon kings, also claiming legitimacy, and perhaps a little deaf to finer points of phonetics, transliterated this to *Bretwald*. The intention is always the same—a claim to rule over *all* Britain (*cf.* p. 109).

Secondly, in the work of unification a decisive factor was the provision of communications, represented by the famous Roman roads. Nothing comparable to them had been seen before: their deep and careful construction, their solid foundation, their surfacing, and the V-shaped ditches on either side for proper drainage. Nothing comparable to them was to be built for many centuries; two names which we still use as synonyms for 'road' (that is 'highway' and 'street') show how they impressed our Anglo-Saxon forefathers. For 'highway' was literally how the Roman road appeared to later eyes—a raised ridge running across the countryside—and 'street' derives from the Latin strata (meaning 'paved'). These roads were designed originally to connect strategic points, garrison forts and camps, and for transporting supplies to them. In the lowland country their breadth might be as much as 18 or even 24 feet; the more mountainous regions were served by narrower pack-horse tracks and patrol-ways (such as 'High Street' over above Ullswater). As the years went on these great trunk roads were supplemented by others, opening up districts to exploitation and commerce in a comprehensive network; where soldiers had once marched travellers and pedlars with their packs could trudge along. So, allowing for certain easily explained exceptions, we may claim that this network is still the basis and foundation for the modern road system of England and Wales. (See Plate 18.) A motorist, setting out from London for Exeter or Gloucester, for Chester or Holyhead or Carlisle, for York or Newcastle, may still ride for miles on a road that runs over the trace of Roman work.

We may mark, next, in connection with communications, how clearly the Romans grasped the right siting for camps, colonies and cities. Such cities and towns as London, Colchester, Chichester, Bath, Winchester, Worcester, Gloucester, Exeter, Lincoln, Chester, York, Lancaster, Carlisle, all go back to an original Roman foundation. If it be noticed that this does not apply to Bristol or Birmingham, Sheffield or Leeds, the answer is that factors emerging long after the departure of the Romans are responsible, such as the discovery of Newfoundland and America and the Industrial Revolution. Remembering too, how great was the use of Roman roads for campaigns in the Dark Ages and early medieval times, we may claim that the Romans had a knack of urbanisation on the right sites and at the important centres.

On the English language the Roman occupation left only a slight impress. But on another tongue still spoken in the island, Welsh, it had a considerable influence. Coming with a more advanced civilisation, the Romans introduced new arts and new inventions, together with the names for them. The easiest way to observe this is by setting out in a parallel column certain Welsh words belonging to different categories, and the Latin words from which they directly derive. (It should be remarked that though most of these Welsh words are still modern parlance all are not, though this does diminish the force of the argument.)

Thus, in farming and land-work we have:

saddle	ystrodur	(*straturam*)
stock	ysgrubl	(*scripulum*)
manger	preseb	(*praesepe*)
pitchfork	fforch	(*furcam*)
bridle	ffrwyn	(*frenum*)
halter	cebystr	(*capistrum*)
well	pydew	(*puteum*)
ladder	ysgol	(*scalam*)
mill	melin	(*molinam*)

In shipping:

ship	llong	(*longam*) *navem*
anchor	angor	(*ancoram*)
oar	rhywf	(*remum*)
harbour	porth	(*portum*)

In building construction:

masonry wall	mur	(*murum*)
partition-wall	pared	(*parietem*)
door-post	post	(*postem*)
transom	trawst	(*transtrum*)
window	ffenestr	(*fenestram*)

Others could be mentioned—for example, ffynnon (*fontanam*), a fountain; tafarn (*tabernam*), a shop or inn; soap (*sebon*) and sponge (*ysbwyng*); names for pots, dishes, pans, and what the French so gracefully call *batterie de cuisine*—but these examples must suffice. The survival of the word for mill in (modern) Welsh is a reminder that the Romans first harnessed the water-power of this island; an archæological proof of this fact, important for economic history, is that traces of the installation of at least three 'undershot' water-mills have been found along the line of the English Wall: at Chesters on the South Tyne, at Haltwhistle Burn, and by Willowford on the River Irthing. Taken together, they bear evidence for the increased mechanical resources that Rome put at the disposal of the inhabitants of Britain, of new developments in farming, in masonry and wood-working, of new arts and refinements, and of the art of cleanliness.

Turning to the soil and its produce, we may remark that it is *a priori* unlikely that a great colonising power would not introduce some of the familiar trees, plants and fruits of the Mediterranean area. Some evidence is already available—and further research should increase it—that that is precisely what the Romans did. The evidence is of various kinds, literary, archæological and linguistic. To begin with the clearest instance, we have a definite statement (Pliny, *Natural History*, xv, 102) that by about the year 50 the cherry-tree had been transplanted to this country, and this is backed up by archæology, in the discovery, in a Roman well, of twigs of the cherry. Further, archæological exploration suggests strongly that not only the cherry, but also the walnut and sweet chestnut, and (from excavations at Caerwent) herbs such as coriander, dill and alexanders, vegetables, *e.g.* the cultivated pea, and flowers such as the poppy, were also introduced into this island during the occupation.

Provisionally we may say that though fig and grape seem to be rare, varieties of apple, cherry, raspberry, strawberry, plum and damson are found on Roman sites during the period of occupation. Dogmatism would be foolhardy, but I believe myself that most of these are Roman importations, while sloes and bullaces (also found) belong to the pre-Roman period. Among flowers we can include poppy, rose and violet; and we know that poppy-seeds were used as a relish on bread (as they still are in Balkan countries). Among vegetables, upon a combination of archæological and linguistic evidence, we can include peas, beans, beet-root and cabbage. Among trees we may list the box, laurel and olive, and, as the plane had reached north France by the middle of the first century, according to Pliny (*Natural History*, xii, 6), it may reasonably be assumed that it crossed the Channel later.

In drawing up such a list I have relied both upon literary and archæological evidence, and that may be regarded as certain. But there is linguistic testimony as well: anyone who takes the trouble to collect and compare the names for common fruits and vegetables in Welsh, Flemish, French and German will at once be struck by the number of them that obviously derive directly from Latin. This derivation cannot be late, for a decree of Charlemagne shows that all these common fruits and vegetables were growing in France by his time. Archæological, literary and linguistic evidence may all fairly be combined in order to produce a picture of Roman Britain, and the results could be checked with the data derivable from Anglo-Saxon herbals.

This topic must not be regarded as of interest only to the botanically-minded. If these contentions are correct (and I believe that the combined work of scholars and scientists can test, and approve or reject them), then we owe a debt both æsthetic and gastronomic to the Romans for certain trees and flowers, fruits and nuts, and in addition we possess data of sociological importance about the diet of those times. If we combine this with the linguistic evidence from Welsh for kitchen implements and tableware, we gain some fresh light upon that phrase, *conviviorum elegantiam*, which Tacitus uses in his life of *Agricola* when he lists the pleasures of a refined table among those arts which the Romans taught our ancestors.

The evidence adduced in the catalogue of Welsh words derived from Latin (p. 93) suggests strongly that the Romans first taught this island the art of carving and cutting stone, either for public buildings or for the private houses of the wealthy, and something of the art of carpentry. It is significant that towards the end of the third century, when the city of Autun needed repair and rebuilding, masons and craftsmen were immediately drafted over from Britain, where there was an abundant supply of trained labour. Even more had Rome taught the art of constructing defensive barriers, great walls or earthworks, and this knowledge survived among their descendants or could be carried by deserters to foreign parts. Many of the post-Roman defensive linear earthworks *look* not unlike a Roman dyke as seen from the outside: the Black Pig's Dyke in Ulster, the Devil's Dyke in East Anglia, and Offa's Dyke (on the Welsh Marches) correspond to that description. Into that category would fall the so-called Roman camp at Bombie, in Kirkcudbrightshire; when it was excavated recently it turned out to be post-Roman, but certainly built by 'people conversant with Roman methods of fortification'.

Another aspect that deserves closer study is that of the importing of animals, and the breeding of Roman with native strains. Here again it may reasonably be assumed that the Romans would introduce new breeds both of sheep and of cattle (as we know, for example, that Columella's father cross-bred sheep in Spain), but the archæological evidence to back such an assumption cannot as yet be called definite. At Newstead camp, on the River Tweed, the earlier excavator found clear traces of three kinds of horse in use: native ponies, better-bred horses measuring about fourteen hands, and powerful large-headed horses. These, and the breeds used for the heavy-armed cavalry of late Roman times, and of the Arthurian and post-Roman age, must have left their mark on the breeding of British horses. But at the moment the evidence is too uncertain to lay down more than possibilities.

Perhaps the Roman's greatest gift was Christianity. It was implanted during their occupation; true, it was afterwards driven out from most of England, but it remained in Wales and Cornwall; and its reintroduction (in Saxon times) came not only from the south-east and from Gallic lands, but also from Ireland, where the efforts of the Romano-Briton, St. Patrick, had established it beyond shaking. Thus the Celtic Christianity of the north can be claimed as a heritage of the Roman occupation. For the existence of Christianity before the Romans withdrew, a passage in Bede (*Ecclesiastical History*, i, 26) tells of an early church at Canterbury, and we know British bishops attended Synods both at Arles in 314 and at Rimini in 359. There was even one early British heretic, Pelagius, and heresy implies the previous existence of orthodoxy. On the archæological side there is evidence for a small church at Silchester, for a still smaller one at Caerleon, and at Cirencester a curious word-square, recently identified as Christian, testifies to the existence there of a Christian community. Nor must we forget smaller objects, such as rings or spoons or pewter vessels, belonging to private owners, bearing the XP which proves those owners to have been Christian. Even though a great deal of organised Christianity was driven out (or underground) in subsequent centuries, St. Patrick had already accomplished his life's work. As a boy he had been kidnapped by Irish pirates raiding up the Solway, who took him back to captivity in Ulster. There he acted as a shepherd-boy on Slemish, near 'the Forest of Foclut, beside the western sea' (the Irish Channel). After six years he made his escape, but was destined ultimately to return and to evangelise thoroughly the country and the people who had once held him captive.

One other point should perhaps be noticed here, even

G

though it may not be strictly relevant to the question of the survivals of Romano-British civilisation: that Britain now becomes for the first time articulate. Before the Roman occupation scholars are compelled to guess what the inhabitants thought and said: from this time onwards, thanks to literary documents or to inscriptions, we know. Is it a Roman general? Tacitus recounts of Agricola how often he had heard him declare (as generals are apt to do, discussing their projects over the nuts and wine), 'that only one Legion and a small force of native troops would be needed for overrunning and then holding down Ireland'. Is it a Caledonian? We know of one, Lossio Veda by name, who served with the Roman forces, and has left behind him, at Colchester (where he was probably concerned with trooping across to the continent), a loyal dedication and a vow for the victory of the emperor Alexander Severus (c. A.D. 225). Or a Roman centurion? An altar dug up from one of the forts of the Scottish Roman Wall shows us M. Cocceius Firmus paying his respects to 'the Spirit that watches over the land of Britain', *genio terrae Britannicae*, and gives us a glimpse of the cautious and tolerant reverence of the Roman soldier towards foreign deities. An otherwise unknown pedlar or traveller, passing through Swaledale, after (let us hope) a successful day's trip, erected an altar to evince his gratitude to 'the god who first thought of roads and paths'. A plain workman inscribes on a tile 'Primus has made ten', or the single word *Satis* ('Time to knock off')—a welcome word to toilers in all ages. From St. Patrick we have a wonderful account of his adventurous and storm-tossed life, one passage of which has always appealed to me so strongly that I must quote it. After his early captivity in Ireland he eventually returned safe and sound to his kinsfolk, who besought him never to leave them again. Yet he could not forget those people over the western sea, among whom he had been a slave. He had many dreams, and in one of them he seemed to see a man coming from the direction of Ireland bearing countless letters. 'One of them he gave to me, and I read the opening of the letter, which was entitled "the voice of the Irish"; and while I was reading aloud the beginning of the letter, I thought I heard, at that very moment, the voice of them that lived beside the Forest of Foclut, which is nigh unto the western sea. And thus they cried as with one mouth, "We beseech thee, holy youth, to come and walk among us once more." And I was exceedingly broken in heart, and could read no further. And so I awoke. . . . Thanks be to God that after many years the Lord granted them according to their cry' (*Confessio*, 23). Soldier or saint, pedlar or workman, henceforward we can read and understand their sentiments.

It is worth summarising what remained.

First, the tradition of Britain as a unity; one country under one ruler, a notion which persisted in Celtic tradition for many centuries, and found its fulfilment when a Welshman, Henry Tudor, ascended the throne of England and Wales.

Second, the existence of a system of communications, which for several centuries afterwards was to regulate commerce and traffic, and to determine both the direction of campaigns and the sites of battles. 'Much the most of the great battles,' writes H. Belloc, 'took place on or near the Roman roads until the twelfth century; most of the great monastic or other houses were built near them, and the ports most commonly used in the Dark Ages were nearly always ports with a Roman road serving them.'

Third, to the Roman occupation we owe the sites of some of our greatest and most famous cities. Their origin is mostly betrayed by names in England ending in -caster, or -cester, or -chester, and in Wales (and in north-western Celtic England) by names beginning with Caer- or Car-, as for example Caernarvon or Carmarthen, or Carlisle, Cardurnock, or Carvoran. It is worth observing, too, how many of them are still important or notable places, and several the sites of bishoprics. Long after the departure of the Romans the memory of the two chief cities of Britain remained at Rome, which explains why Gregory the Great intended London and York to be the sites for the two archbishoprics of the country, and not (as happened) Canterbury and York. In fact, some of the most important sites had been selected by the Romans, and the road connections between them laid down.

Another lasting survival was the influence of Latin upon the Welsh language. Professor Sir Ifor Williams has estimated the number of Latin derivatives in Welsh at about a thousand. Upon analysis they seem to fall into certain definite categories, mostly what might be called 'cultural' categories. These reveal what we might expect, the new things that Rome brought to Britain—the development of sailing and shipping, construction and building in wood or stone (from a fortification to a house or shed), organised farming life, the pleasures of the table, and the greater use of water, whether by wells or fountains or by water-mills. (I have omitted the terms of organised ecclesiastical life, because they may come in much later.) It would be rash to assert that *all* those things which are now called by Latin derivative names were completely new (e.g. *cebystr*=halter), but it looks as though the Romano-British 'natives' learnt them from Latin-speaking masters, who had learnt their Latin at school, and a very classical Latin at that. 'I think we may reasonably imagine,' writes Professor K. H. Jackson, 'the scene of a large country *villa*, where the family often spoke fairly good conservative Latin among themselves, though their native language was British—much as educated Russians used to speak French, and Parisian French, not a *patois*. The slaves and farm hands would speak only British . . . and their masters spoke to them in British. But many Latin words and names for individual things might well be picked up by servants in this way.'

Two matters relating to weights and coinage perhaps merit mention here.

First, 'the commercial pound divided into 16 oz. of 437 grains (identical with the Roman ounce) seems to have been in use before the Conquest, perhaps continuously from Roman times'.

Second, it is worth noting how frequently on the early Anglo-Saxon coins appear two devices, the Eagle or the Twins of Rome: both these devices derive from the Roman coinage, and the intention in the use of them must be a claim to legitimate rule, or at any rate a suggestion that it is still 'the old firm under new management'.

On the subject of importations, of one or two in the plant world we can be quite certain—the cherry, the vine, the sweet chestnut, the poppy and the cabbage; about certain others we may reasonably argue either on the evidence of language or of archæology, or by analogy from other provinces. But there still remains the question of their survival, and that needs serious consideration. It can indeed be argued that in material things such as water-mills or hypocausts, skill and labour and resources were all lacking in the post-Roman ages, and so they fell into ruin for lack of anyone capable of maintaining or repairing them. But it seems hardly likely that invaders would deliberately burn or root up fruit-trees or nut-trees all over the island, and in the west (Cornwall, Wales, Cumbria), once planted, they would have been tended and preserved. On this whole question we may hope for great advances in the future.

Last, there was the introduction of Christianity, for which there is definite evidence from literary sources. The visible remains may be slight, but how few Romano-British towns have been thoroughly explored, of how few have we a reliable street plan! We can safely trust the literary evidence, and hope for confirmation (and possibly for surprising discoveries) from archæology in the future. These British Christians, whether saints and evangelists, such as St. Patrick, or sages, such as the wise Gildas, or heretics, such as Pelagius, had learnt their Latin; they were proud to think of themselves still as Romans, and to call Latin 'our language'. Their writings and their art, whether surviving in Wales or transplanted to Ireland, form no inconsiderable portion of the influence that the Roman occupation of Britain exerted on later generations.

These, then, are the main elements, some of them material and visible, some intangible and spiritual, in the heritage which the Romans bequeathed to the Saxon conquerors and settlers in our island, and so through them to us in the present day. The list is not exhaustive, but even in this shortened form it may serve to show that the occupation did not vanish leaving 'not a rack behind', but left something enduring in this island and in the blood of the inhabitants of the land to-day.

SUGGESTIONS FOR FURTHER READING

M. P. Charlesworth, *The Lost Province or the Worth of Britain*, Cardiff, 1949. (This book sets out more fully the views expressed in the chapter.)

R. G. Collingwood, *Roman Britain* (with plates and a map), 1932.

R. G. Collingwood and J. N. L. Myres, *Roman Britain and the English Settlements*, 1936, 2nd ed. 1937.

C. Fox, *The Personality of Britain*, Cardiff, 1932; 4th ed. revised, 1943.

F. J. Haverfield and G. Macdonald, *The Roman Occupation of Britain*, 1924.

T. C. Lethbridge, *Merlin's Island*, 1948.

I. A. Richmond, *Roman Britain* (Britain in Pictures Series), 1947.

Hugh Williams, *Christianity in Early Britain*, 1912.

V

NORA K. CHADWICK

The Celtic West

THE Celtic period, or more generally the Celtic
West, has special reference, roughly speaking,
to the period from the close of the fourth to the seventh
century, with an extension to the eighth, and even to
the ninth, when we come to discuss the Celtic Church.
It is, however, important to remember that the vast
majority of Englishmen and Englishwomen are the
direct descendants of a population, which had probably
been speaking some form of Celtic language for nearly
fifteen hundred years when the first Saxons disembarked
from the continent of Europe. The language which
we speak in England to-day is, of course, not a Celtic
but a Teutonic language. This is due to the fact that
the Saxons gained the upper hand of the Celtic-speaking
people of England. But though the Saxons were
vigorous and daring they cannot have been very
numerous, for they came in ships. A contemporary
writer tells us that to them shipwreck was just so much
practice, and they are never stated to have brought
their women with them.

Even to-day, if we look at a map of the British Isles,
we shall see that the Celtic area is more than half of it.
It is, from every point of view, a matter of the first
importance that we should realise our debt to the Celtic

culture of past ages, and what it is in our present civilisation that has come to us from our direct Celtic-speaking ancestors and our present Celtic neighbours. What are the features which are most outstanding and most valuable in the Celtic culture? I shall try to answer this question briefly by looking at Celtic Britain in perspective, and at a period when the Celtic-speaking peoples were playing an all-important part in the history of our islands—when the Roman power was already waning, and the Saxons were just making a new home for themselves here from across the North Sea.

The struggle between Saxon and Celt for the supremacy in our islands may be said to begin, in a political and military sense, before the Romans left, when the first boat-loads of Saxons were disembarking in the fifth century A.D.; and to close in the ninth century, when the form of Christianity which St. Augustine gave us gradually brought the earlier form of Celtic Christianity to an end. To all intents and purposes the Saxons took over south-eastern Britain from the Romans. They entered, as we might say, by the front door, and occupied the best rooms of our house. The Celts had to be satisfied with the back premises and the north wing. Their accommodation was more spacious than that of the Saxons, but less comfortable, and very poorly furnished.

During the Roman period, therefore, and still more after the Saxons had settled in England, the British Isles formed two cultural areas. That of central and southern England is virtually identical with the continent, and forms an area homogeneous with it. But north and west of this area, including Ireland, is a totally different single area, of which the British portion is something in the nature of a highland zone—a Celtic area. In both areas the true cultural units are not formed by the land but by the sea. In the Celtic West this is especially clear when we stand on one of the promontories of south-western Scotland and look across to the coasts of Cumberland, Ireland and the Isle of Man, stretched out like a relief map round a great Celtic pond. The coracle, or little Celtic boat made of hides stretched over a wicker frame, could ply between these shores far more quickly and easily than a bicycle or a motor-car in the country behind. It is just the same between Wales and Southern Ireland. All our heathen traditions, all our Christian records, speak of easy and constant coming and going across this Celtic pond.

In the land area of Britain east and north of the Celtic pond long-distance communication can only have been easy along the lines of the Roman roads and the Roman Walls. The northern turf Wall—the Antonine Wall, stretching from the Firth of Forth to the Firth of Clyde—played a very important part in early Celtic history. This Wall is the waist-line of Scotland—a 'wasp waist'. It is Scotland's most restricted point, only about thirty-seven miles wide from east to west. The ease of communication between the two extremities made it easy to patrol and defend the entire length, and determined the future of our country.

The Celts of the fifth century, like the modern Celts, were divided into various groups and spoke differing dialects. In the centre and north of Scotland—north, that is to say, of the Antonine Wall—were the strong and warlike Picts, probably the oldest of the Celtic-speaking peoples of Britain who maintained their identity down to historical times. They had a number of kingdoms, with powerful kings and a fleet of their own. In historical times the Northern Picts had their centre at Inverness, and the Southern Picts were divided into four kingdoms around the Firth of Tay. Their culture was surprisingly high. We have many references to the 'ancient books of the Picts', whatever this means precisely. At any rate they kept the records of their kings from very early times, and they were never conquered.

South of the Picts—south, that is, of the Antonine Wall—were the British, who were known to later Welsh tradition as the *Gwyr y Gogledd*, the 'Men of the North'. They were closely related to the Welsh of Wales and Cornwall. In the fifth century these British or Welsh-speaking peoples were forming themselves into a number of kingdoms, which stretched from the Firth of Forth, through Cumberland, Lancashire and Wales to Devonshire and Cornwall and even to Brittany. There was only one language spoken throughout the whole area. A traveller from Edinburgh to St. Malo would have been able to converse freely with the inhabitants the whole way.

It is generally, though not universally, held that some form of Gaelic must have been spoken in Britain before the establishment of Welsh. But recent Celtic scholars think that the Gaelic spoken in Scotland to-day probably came into Scotland from Ireland about the fifth century through the kingdom of Argyll, which was founded and colonised from Ireland about this time. If this is so, we must believe that the kings of Argyll, like the Saxon rulers of England, gradually imposed their language throughout the whole of the country. The royal house of Argyll intermarried with the Picts of Inverness, and Kenneth mac Alpin, the king of Argyll, succeeded in uniting Scotland under one rule about the middle of the ninth century, and the Pictish and the British (Welsh) languages disappeared from Scotland (see Plate 19).

Towards the close of the Roman period the British kingdoms of southern Scotland and western England had become largely Romanised, and were entrusted by the Romans with the defences of southern Britain against the hostile Celtic peoples to the north and west (see p. 89). The leaders bore Roman names, and sometimes Roman epithets implying Roman distinction or office. They must have been trained in Roman traditional methods of warfare, and were probably supplied with Roman arms and Roman money. By the early fifth century, and perhaps earlier, these Romanised British kingdoms formed powerful buffer states, and were able to confine the Picts to the north of the Antonine Wall, and to ensure for southern Britain a kind of *pax Britannica*.

These kingdoms were probably in the nature of loose confederacies, for the people were still in an 'Heroic Age' of society. There was no strong central government, no written legal code, no urban life, no general currency, no organised industries, and a fairly low standard of material culture. The only notable form of architecture which has survived above ground is the stone and earthen ramparts of their fortifications and 'hilltop cities'. There were many rulers, kings and princes, sometimes referred to in our Latin sources as *subreguli*. But all kings were absolute so far as they could enforce their power, and from time to time an important ruler made himself supreme over a number of smaller kings and established a hereditary dynasty.

In Ireland, the ruling member of the most important dynasty was known as the *ard-rí*, the 'High King'. In Wales, the name *Vortigern*, by which we know the great ruler of the buffer state on the Welsh border in the fifth century, is in reality a title and means 'chief lord' (*ver-tigernas*). The term *gwledig* attached to the names of some British princes implies that the owner held special powers of this kind, and the Anglo-Saxon title *Bret-walda* is probably derived from this, both in meaning and function. Bede's description of the Pictish king of Inverness in the sixth century as *rex potentissimus*, 'a specially powerful king', may be a translation of *vortigern* (*ver-tigernas*) or *ard-rí*.

Vortigern is perhaps the greatest British name in fifth-century history. According to the official pedigree he began life by marrying Sevira, the daughter of the Emperor Maximus, known to later Welsh tradition as *Maxen Gwledig*. But when Maximus left Britain in 383, taking the Roman troops with him, Vortigern seems to have adopted an anti-Roman policy and a romantic nationalism—'Britain for the British'. We are told that he 'loved his country', and that he 'feared' Ambrosius Aurelianus, apparently a Romano-British military leader fighting successfully for the Roman cause in the south-west of England. By joining forces with the Saxons who landed in Kent, Vortigern drove a wedge between the Roman powers in the south-west and those centred at York, isolating Ambrosius and his forces, and cutting them off from supplies. Strategically he could have dealt no more effective blow to the Roman power in Britain.

About this time we hear of a great military movement made by the sons of a certain British chief, Cunedda Gwledig, from the neighbourhood of

Edinburgh, into North Wales, probably to check the Irish settlements there, which were becoming very formidable, and the threat of a full-scale Irish invasion in western Wales or north-western England. The 'Sons of Cunedda' settled permanently in Wales, giving it the name by which they themselves were known, *Cymry*, 'compatriots', the name which survives in the modern Cumberland. In Wales they formed a number of small dynasties, ruling each his own kingdom, many of them forming the nucleus of the modern Welsh counties. The course of events suggests that as Roman power waned the British buffer states in the north and west formed some sort of alliance, and seized the moment of Roman weakness to get rid of them once and for all, and to re-establish the British supremacy of Britain.

It was largely the break-down of the unity of the British kingdoms during the sixth century which gave the Saxons their chance of a large-scale occupation. Even King Arthur and his twelve victorious battles against the Saxons, even all the heroic battles fought by the 'Men of the North' and commemorated for centuries in the poems of the Welsh bards, could not save Britain when disunion among the British became serious. Had the co-operation of the British states broken down earlier, the Picts would certainly have stepped in and prevented the Saxons from obtaining a foothold. The Southern Picts under their king Brude mac Bile were still a strong power, able to repel the Saxon invasion by the Northumbrian king Ecgfrith north of the Tay in 685—because, as a Pictish bard triumphantly sang,

'God favoured Brude mac Bile.'

And on the other hand, if British organisation and

co-operation had lasted longer, the British could themselves have prevented the Saxon occupation. After all, only as many Saxons could come here as their ships could carry.

Wales did not become a united nation till about a century later than Scotland. Then the great Welsh king, Hywel the Good, united himself with the English king. His death is recorded in 950. He recognised the value of a coinage and a charter, and had the ancient Welsh laws written down from the lips of the trained legislators and officials who had been responsible for carrying them on and administering them by word of mouth. The Welsh laws, like the Irish, make very good reading, and give us an intimate insight into the rights and privileges of the Welsh courts. Even the clothing allowances and the food rations of the court officials are intimately set down. And we hear of the duties of the bards. The household bard, for instance, must sing to the queen in her chamber whenever she wishes; 'but he must sing softly lest the hall be disturbed'.

Perhaps the most engaging entry is the penalty for killing a cat which guards the king's barn:

'Whoever shall kill a cat which guards the king's barn, or shall take it stealthily, its head is to be held downwards on a clean, level floor, and its tail is to be held upwards; and after that wheat must be poured over it until the tip of its tail is hidden, and that is its value.'

Really the Welsh laws are a compendium of all kinds of useful or important information. Lest anyone should be ignorant of the points of a well-bred cat, the legislator specifies clearly:

'The points of a cat are that it should be perfect of

ear, perfect of eye, perfect of tail, perfect of teeth, perfect of claw, without marks of fire, and that it should kill mice, and not devour its kittens, and that it should not go caterwauling every full moon.' (See Plate 21.)

The early Britons are probably the only people who treat their laws in a spirit of light humour.

We must not measure Celtic civilisation by the standard of its material culture. The intellectual level was much higher. The Celtic West, the Highland zone of Britain, is beautiful and poor, with mountains and lakes and forests and moors, but not much agriculture, not many industries. So it has always been. And so the early Celts, like the Scots and the Irish and the Welsh to-day, developed a high idealism and a great sense of intellectual values rather than any spectacular material culture. They had inherited fine traditions from the far past which they had carefully cherished and cultivated, and of which they were very proud. And an extraordinarily rich intellectual life was carried on by word of mouth, both in the form of poetry and prose.

This oral tradition was cultivated and preserved by professional poets and prose saga-tellers. There were bards who composed court poetry, panegyrics and elegies on the great chiefs, and poems celebrating great events and battles, and these poems formed the nucleus of the events recorded in the later chronicles. But there was also poetry in a lighter vein. Sir Ifor Williams has translated for us a medieval Welsh poem which was perhaps composed as a lullaby by the household bard:

> The mantle of Dinogat is of many colours,
> From the skins of martens I made it.
> When thy father went a-hunting,

With spear on shoulder, and cudgel in hand,
He would call his big dogs,
    'Giff, Gaff; Catch, Catch; Fetch, Fetch!'
In his coracle he would spear a fish,
Striking suddenly like a lion.
When thy father went up the mountain
He would bring back a roebuck, a wild boar, a stag,
A spotted grouse from the mountains,
A fish from the falls. . . .
None would escape, except those which had wings.

The intellectual poetry and all native learning was in the hands of a class of poets known in Ireland as *filid*, who claimed to give their instruction and pronouncements by supernatural inspiration, and to be able to bring on a poetical trance by a prescribed recipe. This belief in poetic inspiration as a living reality is characteristic of all the Celtic peoples. But the *filid* were also a really learned class in the native oral traditions. They are said to have had a very long and elaborate training, and it is probably ultimately to them that we owe the preservation of a vast wealth of prose saga literature from early Ireland, and the foundations of historical records. A great Irish codex and collection of early literature observes: 'He is no *fili* ("poet"), who does not synchronise and harmonise all the stories.'

The Irish have preserved many piquant and amusing stories of the gods who lived in the great mounds of the ancient dead, and who united under their divine leaders to prevent Ireland from being invaded by a formidable race of supernatural beings from the Scottish islands—men in form, but furnished with three rows of teeth. The gods have their divine family and their skilled craftsmen. When the god Nuadu lost his hand in battle, the divine physician, Diancecht,

H

supplied him with a silver hand. Diancecht was so skilled in surgery that he could replace a man's eye by a cat's eye; but the surgery functioned in Irish fashion, humorously, and only too well; for by day the eye could never keep open, while by night, when the man wanted to sleep, it would start at every squeak of a mouse and every rustle of the reeds.

In Celtic countries there is no epic poetry, but we have an astonishing amount of heroic saga or traditional prose stories. It is the literature of a world of long ago, of an age of individualism, of heroes, of romance and of adventure, in the forests of Ireland, in the lochs of the western Highlands, on the mountains of Wales— Irish stories of King Conchobar of Ulster and his champion Cuchulainn, and their warfare with Queen Medb of Connaght; and stories of Finn, grandson of Nuadu, and Welsh stories of Gwynn ap Nydd who seems to be the same hero. In Welsh tradition Gwynn carries off Creiddylad (Cordelia) after she has been betrothed to Gwythyr ap Greidawl (Victor, son of Gratialis)—an interesting tradition of a feud between a purely Celtic hero and a Roman rival. And the Welsh medieval collection of stories known as the *Mabinogion* contains many traditions of King Arthur which are unrecorded by Geoffrey of Monmouth.

And still in the great days of the Celtic Church the Celtic peoples reverenced their ancient and beautiful stories and poems, and wrote them down in the monasteries alongside the records of their newer Christian learning, and the sweet and simple lives of the Celtic saints. Perhaps no other people in the world, certainly no other Christian people, have shown so broad-minded a tolerance for the heroes and the seers, the magic and mythology of their heathen age, combined with deep Christian fervour and austerity.

The attitude of mind is aptly illustrated in a little ancient Irish poem:

> When I am among my elders,
> I am proof that sport is forbidden;
> When I am among the mad young folk,
> They think that I am their junior.

Ancient Irish stories tell of the visits of the early kings to a supernatural palace in the spirit world. They are led there in a kind of prophetic vision by a ghostly warrior or a god. On a throne inside the palace is a beautiful lady who calls herself the Sovereignty of Ireland, and she gives the king wine from a cauldron beside her, and with every drink which she ladles out, she names to him one of his own descendants. The cauldron is the cauldron of poetic inspiration, and the story seems to represent the king's initiation into manhood and into the 'sovereignty of Ireland'. It is characteristic of the Celtic peoples that the kings should be initiated into the sovereignty in a spiritual *milieu*, and the story is a happy illustration of the high status of women in all the Celtic countries, and of the high regard—the paramount regard—in which poetry is held. It is also an illustration of the whimsical convention of the early Celtic peoples of relating history— in this case the dynastic line of the Irish kings—by prophecy rather than by retrospect.

These prophetic histories no doubt originated in the heathen learning of the *filid*, and they are found in Wales as well as in Ireland; but the favourite native Celtic historical convention was that of necromancy. The greatest Irish heroic saga, 'The Cattle Raid of Cualnge', claims to have been recovered from the past and recited by Fergus mac Roich long after his death; he had taken a prominent part in the cattle raid himself. Similarly St. Patrick and his Christian companions heard the story of Finn mac Cumaill and his followers from one of Finn's warriors whom Patrick had raised from his funeral mound for the purpose.

In Celtic Britain the druids lingered on in the native traditions long after they had been forgotten in Gaul. But we never hear of them in association with heathen religion. Indeed we know little of Celtic heathen religion as distinct from mythology, and we never hear of heathen temples or of organised religious functions or worship, though there are traditions of sanctuaries at the sources of the Shannon and the Boyne. Adamnan records more than one contest between St. Columba and the *magus* Broichan, who was probably a druid, at the Pictish court of Inverness. On the other hand some of the earliest saints, such as St. Brigit, and her spiritual instructor St. Mochtua of Louth, are said to have been brought up in the households of druids, and history records no serious clash between heathenism and Christianity.

In Britain, Christianity had probably had a continuous history from Roman times. St. Patrick reproaches the Picts for being, not pagan, but 'apostate', and he himself belonged to a Romano-British Christian family, probably from south-western Scotland. In Wales, the claim made by tradition for the continuity of the British Church from Roman times is widespread and consistent, and rests ultimately on the excellent preservation of the Welsh genealogies. But there is other evidence.

We possess a document from Ireland in the eighth century known as the *Catalogue of the Saints of Ireland.*

Here the saints are divided into three Orders. The First Order consists of those who received their services from St. Patrick, and its organisation was episcopal. The Second Order of Saints is said to be derived from 'holy men of Britain', from the disciples of St. Illtud, founder of the great monastic School of Llantwit Major in South Wales. This Order was monastic both in character and organisation, but each monastery was quite independent, and there was no central organisation. The Third Order of Saints are those described as 'dwelling in desert places, living on herbs and water and alms, and possessing nothing of their own'. They developed from the Second Order, and became known later as the Culdees. The classification is useful, though its chronological divisions cannot be pressed. The Second Order may have preceded the first.

It is the Saints of the Second Order who gave the Celtic Church the distinctive features which marked it off from the Roman Church of later times, such as the computation of the date of Easter; the Celtic form of the tonsure; special features in the baptismal rite; peculiarities in the liturgy; and, most important of all, the monastic form of Church government. These are technical matters; but the more fundamental, and the more deeply interesting characteristics of the Celtic Church, are its great devotion to learning; its love of wandering and of pilgrimage; its practice of severe austerities and asceticism; and its emphasis on the spiritual, as distinct from the formal, observances of the religious life. And of all these perhaps the most remarkable is the love of learning. The earliest famous ecclesiastical quarrel is about a book—the copy of the Psalms which St. Columba had borrowed from St. Finnian of Moville and which he pirated. The earliest curse on record is also about a book—the curse pronounced by St. Ronan on Suibhne Geilt, because Suibhne had thrown St. Ronan's sacred book into the water. A similar story is told of the Welsh scholar Yscolan in an early Welsh poem.

The great love of learning in the Celtic Church is especially remarkable when we consider the difficulties of the time—with Gaul under a barbarian occupation, and England in process of the Saxon invasions and settlements. Yet the Celtic, and especially the Irish, scholars of the Second Order of Saints did much to keep classical learning alive in western Europe through those devastating times. It was largely Irish pilgrims, and monks in monasteries in France and Italy, who occupied themselves with copying the classics and ensuring their preservation; and the great Irish scholar-saints of the Second Order have made us their debtors for all time, not only for the preservation of these classical texts, but also for the foundation of several of the great continental libraries and schools of learning, 'the very mention of which', says Norden, 'makes the heart of the classical scholar throb'. The journey of Columbanus and his companions in the sixth century from Ireland, through France to Italy, founding monastic schools along their route, hardly falls short of an ecclesiastical Odyssey.

The most remarkable thing about the learning of the Irish Church is its catholicity in the widest sense—the fact that, while absorbing Latin learning, they never abandoned their own traditional culture. The Celtic peoples were alone in northern Europe in eagerly seeking this new Christian Latin learning, and at the same time using the new art of writing to make a deathless record of their own ancient traditions—their poetry, their sagas, their heroic stories, their lists of kings and their histories. They wrote enormous manuscripts containing everything which happened to interest them, both religious and secular—poems and stories, saints' lives and laws, and their extremely complicated rules for metre. These manuscripts served as miniature libraries. Some of them were written in monasteries and by monks, but their contents are even more secular than ecclesiastical. The earliest we know of contained the repertoire of a poet—his 'book of words', as it were.

We know something of the way in which the manuscripts were put together, because the writers had a charming way of scribbling their thoughts in the margins. They are delightfully casual and personal. One scribe writes—probably from Ireland or Britain— with a sense of relief that the weather makes enemy attack by night impossible:

> Bitter is the wind to-night—
> It tosses the ocean's white hair;
> To-night I fear not the fierce warriors of Norway
> Coursing on the Irish Sea.

These early saints realised very well the sacrifice of sunshine and the open air which the scholar's life entails, and one has expressed it with a startling poignancy, scribbling in the margin of a manuscript of Cassiodorus on the Psalms: 'Pleasant is the sunlight to-day upon these margins, because it flickers so.' As Dr. Flower observes, it is the emotion, not the sun, that matters here, and the queer impulse that prompts the record.

Writing is still a new art, painfully learned, and the scribe watches his hand with astonishment as it turns his thoughts into strange little hieroglyphs on the

unsullied page, which he almost seems to regret inking.
All the same he scribbles in the margin:

> My hand is weary with writing,
> My sharp quill is not steady.
> My slender-beaked pen pours forth
> A black draught of shining dark-blue ink.
>
> My little dripping pen travels
> Across the plain of shining books
> Without ceasing, for the wealth of the great;
> Whence my hand is weary with writing.

As one reads these personal poems of the Irish saints
one is conscious of a direct expression of humanity
which, despite their spirituality, is strangely modern.
The emotion is felt with an intensity, and at the same
time viewed with a detachment and expressed with a
clarity that leave an image as pure in line as a cameo
or a gem. The scribe's complaint of the flightiness
of his thoughts might have been written yesterday:

Shame to my thoughts, how they stray from me!
I fear great danger from it on the day of eternal Doom.

During the Psalms they wander on a path that is not right:
They fash, they fret; they misbehave before the eyes of great God.

Through eager crowds, through companies of wanton women,
Through woods, through cities—swifter they are than the wind.

Now through paths of loveliness, anon of riotous shame!
They run a race of folly anear and afar!
After a course of giddiness they return to their home. . . .

Though one should try to bind them or put shackles on their feet,
They are neither constant nor mindful to take a spell of rest. . . .

As slippery as an eel's tail they glide out of my grasp.

But one realises how dearly these scholars valued their

learning. One has jotted down his little impromptu elegy on the death of a fellow scholar:

> Dead is Lon of Kilgarrow.
>   O great hurt!
> To Ireland and beyond her border
>   It is ruin of study and of Schools.

The early ideals and austerities of the Celtic Church perhaps attained their fullest expression in the Culdee movement, which began about the seventh century, and reached its highest development in the eighth and ninth. We can still find traces of their tiny settlements on the islands all round our coast (see Plates 20*a* and 20*b*). Even the stern Gildas, speaking in the sixth century to his enemy Maelgwn, King of Gwynedd in North Wales, softens into a vein of real poetry as he reminds him of his retreat in earlier life in one of these cells:

'Did you not,' Gildas cries, 'by your own will snatch yourself like a dove which in flight from the raven cleaves the thin air with its rustling pinions, and by its rapid turns escapes the speedy hawk with cruel talons, and so safely reached the cells of the saints?'

The mode of life, the daily routine and spiritual discipline, and the kind of environment suited to the austerities of the recluse, is sketched for us in a little anonymous poem of the ninth century:

> I wish, O Son of the living God, O ancient, eternal King,
> For a hidden little hut in the wilderness, that it may be my
>   dwelling. . . .
>
> Quite near, a beautiful wood around it on every side,
> To nurse many-voiced birds, hiding it with its shelter.
>
> A Southern aspect for warmth, a little brook across its floor,
> A choice land with many gracious gifts such as be good for every
>   plant.

This is the husbandry I would take, I would choose, and I will
  not hide it:
Fragrant leeks, hens, salmon, trout, bees. . . .

And I to be sitting for a while praying God in every place.

In these little poems we see the Celtic recluses in
their retreats at one with the little things of nature, not
as chance visitors to the country, but as those who—
again I quote Dr. Flower—'brought to their environment of wood and sea an eye washed miraculously
clear by a continual spiritual exercise, so that they,
first in Europe, had that strange vision of natural
things in an almost unnatural purity'.

Perhaps this close touch with nature, and the living
things of the country-side, helps to explain why in the
Celtic Church the spirit never grew harsh or the self-
discipline formal or rigid. Purity of spirit is always
stressed as more important than external observance.
In the margin of a ninth-century codex at Berne,
written in an entirely Irish hand, we read:

> To go to Rome
> Is much of trouble and little of profit:
> The King whom thou seekest there,
> Unless thou bring Him with thee, thou wilt not find.

Another queer little personal marginal poem:

> Sweet little bell
> That is struck in the windy night,
> I had liefer go to a tryst with thee
> Than to a tryst with a foolish woman.

The gentle humanity and sympathy of these Irish
poems, and their brilliant wit, is seen at its height in
the little eighth- or ninth-century satire of the studious
monk and his pet cat Pangur, whose concentration on
his own pursuits of mousing, and whose superior skill

in his art the monk wistfully compares with his own fumbling efforts to bring clarity out of obscurity in his scholarly problems:

> I and my White Pangur
> Have each his special art:
> His mind is set on hunting mice,
> Mine is upon my special craft.
>
> I love to rest—better than any fame!—
> At close study with my little book;
> White Pangur does not envy me:
> He loves his childish play. . . .
>
> He rejoices with quick leaps
> When in his sharp claw sticks a mouse:
> I too rejoice when I have grasped
> A problem difficult and dearly loved.
>
> Though we are thus at all times,
> Neither hinders the other,
> Each of us, pleased with his own art,
> Amuses himself alone.

It is easy to see why the Celtic Church was so averse to strife and quarrelling and why it never had any persecutions. And although the later reformed Church which St. Augustine introduced into England ultimately superseded the earlier Celtic Church in the seventh and eighth centuries, the old spirit remained to leaven and sweeten the men and the organisation which were superimposed. Even the Venerable Bede, ardent and zealous as he was for reform and orthodoxy, eager as he was to see the Celtic Church give way to the Church Universal, yet pays the handsomest tribute of all to the humility and dignity, the simplicity and sincerity, and above all the utter unworldliness of the Celtic saints of his day, and of his own personal acquaintance.

It is probably no overstatement to say that intellectual life reached a higher level in our country during the Anglo-Saxon period than for many centuries later. But this culture had its roots still deeper in the intellectual achievements of the Celts. A little Anglo-Saxon poem on the ruins of Roman Bath pictures a descendant of the Saxon invaders gazing on the havoc made by his ancestors which he knows only as 'masonry shattered by Fate, buildings raised of old by giants'. How different and how enlightened is the Celtic attitude to Roman Carlisle of which we get a glimpse in Bede's Life of St. Cuthbert, where the saint awaits news of King Ecgfrith's battle against the Picts, and in the interval is taken by the citizens of Carlisle on a conducted tour 'to see the walls of the city, and a marvellously constructed fountain of Roman workmanship'. How modern this sounds!

The extent to which our Anglo-Saxon culture is rooted in the past has never been fully appreciated. The great Anglo-Saxon scholar Alcuin, head of the palace school of Charlemagne, corresponded in terms of deep respect with an Irish monk, Colcu in York. A generation earlier the great Aldhelm, abbot of Malmesbury and the founder of its famous library, was trained in the Irish tradition. The great school of learning in Northumbria, of which Bede is the brightest jewel, was built up on the earlier foundations laid by King Aldfrith, who had received his education in Celtic lands. King Alfred the Great was brought up in an area which was still predominantly Celtic. He persuaded the bishop of St. David's to act as his chief adviser. He took a leading part in the affairs of the Welsh Church and in Welsh politics. He contributed to the funds of the Irish Church. And the death of a famous Irish scholar caused three Irish pilgrims to cross the Irish sea in a little coracle, and to make their way to Alfred's court and bring him the news—a solitary Irish *obit* in our Saxon Chronicle. They must have had good reason to know that this loss to Irish scholarship would be of interest to King Alfred. Indeed Alfred was as much a Celt in his love of learning as in the burning of the cakes.

King Aldfrith of Northumbria and King Alfred the Great are undoubtedly the two most intellectual kings in the history of England, and it is important that their Celtic milieu should be realised. I believe that it was largely due to his Celtic background and Celtic interests that King Alfred was the first Anglo-Saxon scholar to emphasise the importance of translating Latin works into the vernacular. The most interesting of the shorter Anglo-Saxon poems, a little group of personal and elegiac anonymous poems contained in a great manuscript preserved in Exeter Cathedral, is probably of direct Celtic inspiration, especially the poems called the Wanderer and the Seafarer which tell of a life at sea. They are unique in Saxon literature, and more than a century of scholarship has failed to ascertain their poetical milieu. But they are essentially the poetry associated in Celtic countries with the Culdees or *peregrini*, the recluses and 'pilgrims' of the Celtic Church who wandered over Europe, carrying their learning abroad, and composed the richest body of poetry of any Christian Church. Our unique MS of the great Anglo-Saxon epic *Beowulf* was probably transcribed at Lichfield, and again in Celtic surroundings.

It is not to our Celtic ancestors that we owe our most impressive monuments of the past, nor our outstanding capacity for trade, nor our advanced urban system and political constitution. Our debt to them is intellectual and poetical. They give us a passport and a safe-conduct into the world of the imagination, and their greatest heirloom is their poetry. Following on an age of order and of high material culture under the Romans, the Celtic period in Britain comes as our first Romantic Revival. It is the most romantic period in our history, the age when poetry was most highly cultivated and held in greatest reverence. It is a period of individualism and of dominating personalities, and of great poets whose names have come down to us for nearly 1,500 years. It is an age of idealism, with a full intellectual and spiritual life, marked by passionate love of liberty, love of home-land, hatred of a foreign domination, despite the attractions of a higher standard of living and of material culture. It is the age in which all the spiritual values to which we cling most passionately to-day were born.

I would define our legacy from Celtic Britain briefly thus. By their affection for their own ancient traditions, and their careful recording of their native Celtic literature, side by side with the newer Latin learning, they have given us a sense of the importance of the past and the value of continuity as the best inspiration for the future. At the same time, by their devotion to scholarship, they have preserved much ancient manuscript material which must otherwise have perished, and they have bequeathed to us a tradition of devoted study throughout a period of destructive barbarism and harassing wars. The Anglo-Roman Church on which our own is founded was deeply influenced by the unworldliness of the Celtic Church, and by its firm hold on spiritual values in religion—its charity and humility, its simplicity and humour, and its deep and intense affection for little homely things.

Both their religious and their personal poetry is marked by a refinement of feeling and a sympathy which is incompatible with persecution or cruelty, and which puts integrity and kindness above all formal standards of conduct. Perhaps the most remarkable of the Celtic gifts to us is the awakening of the individual to an interest in himself, and the realisation of the importance of personality. The Celts, first among our ancestors, have spoken to us as individuals through their poems and their prose. They first discovered for us the range and significance of individual experience, and the interest and the humour of little personal things, and how exciting and valuable it is to share them with one another.

SUGGESTIONS FOR FURTHER READING

A. H. Williams, *An Introduction to the History of Wales*, Vol I, Cardiff, 1941.

W. F. Skene, *Celtic Scotland*, 3 vols., Edinburgh, 1890.

Hugh Williams, *Christianity in Early Britain*, 1912.

R. Flower, *The Irish Tradition*, 1947.

Sir Ifor Williams, *Lectures on Early Welsh Poetry*, Dublin, 1944.

M. Dillon, *The Cycles of the Kings*, 1946.

M. Dillon, *Early Irish Literature*, Chicago, 1948.

A. W. Wade-Evans, *Welsh Medieval Law*, 1909.

Lady Charlotte Guest, *The Mabinogion* (Everyman's Library, Temple Classics, etc.).

T. P. Cross and C. H. Slover, *Ancient Irish Tales*, New York, 1936.

K. H. Jackson, *A Celtic Miscellany*, 1951.

VI

PETER HUNTER BLAIR

The Foundations
of England

MORE than six hundred years lie between the departure of the Romans from Britain and the arrival of the Normans in England. To justify the use of a title which has been borrowed from a nineteenth century historian, it need only be remarked that this was the period within which England first took shape, within which the English language first came to be used in Britain, and within which the English people first received the faith which they still profess.

This span of time may seem short in comparison with archæological ages, yet the departure of the Romans was no less remote from the Norman Conquest than was the battle of Hastings from the restoration of Charles II. Some help towards understanding the significance of this long period of English history will perhaps be gained from distinguishing three main phases within it, each broadly equal in time: first, a period of invasion and settlement extending from the end of Roman rule; second, an intermediate phase in which the earliest English society developed; and third, a period of renewed external attack, coming this time from Scandinavia and culminating in the conquest of

England by the Normans, themselves a people of Scandinavian descent.

The effect of the Roman withdrawal was to place Britain, or rather England, as much of it very soon became, outside the Latin countries, to tie her more closely to north-western Europe and less closely to Mediterranean civilisation. But this is to take the long view, and if anyone were to ask what was the immediate effect of the withdrawal upon the people of Britain themselves, he might find an important part of his answer in the reply sent by the emperor Honorius to a British appeal for help against foreign invaders (see p. 89). He answered, in effect, that the British must now fight for themselves.

For nearly four hundred years the population of Roman Britain had enjoyed the protection of an almost invincible professional army, but that army had now gone, and if the British were to maintain their independence they must either take up arms themselves or seek help elsewhere. There is evidence, amongst which the legend of Arthur is not unimportant, that both these measures were adopted with some initial success. Both English and Welsh tradition, represented in part by the familiar story of Hengist and Horsa, alleges that the English first came to Britain at the invitation of the British, and that they engaged to fight Britain's enemies in return for lands on which they could settle. According to Gildas, a Welsh writer, the experiment succeeded at first, but the English soon rebelled and conquered the country which they had come to defend. The truth of these traditions cannot now be established, but it is likely enough that the British sought to escape from their troubles by using the enemies who attacked them from one side against those who threatened from the other.

The name by which the English call both themselves and the country in which they live is derived from a Germanic tribal name, *Engle*, that of a seemingly small and undistinguished people who lived near the neck of the Jutland peninsula between Schleswig and Flensburg, where the modern name Angeln is thought still to preserve their memory. The *Engle*, or *Angli* as Latin writers called them, were however only one of several Germanic peoples who invaded Britain in the fifth century. Mingled with them were Saxons, Frisians and Jutes, the first two coming from between the Elbe and the Rhine mouths, and the last from a locality which has never been firmly established. Both before and during the invasion period there was no doubt a considerable intermingling of peoples, and the study of language, as well as of social and economic organisation in later times, reveals such a degree of uniformity over much of England as to suggest that earlier tribal distinctions between Angles, Saxons and Frisians had been very largely obliterated in that general movement of peoples during what is called the Migration Period.

Although the territory which was occupied by the Jutes, mainly Kent, shows certain distinctive features, the invaders who established themselves over most of the lowland area of Britain were a mixed population which can conveniently be called Anglo-Saxon, a compound term which first came into use on the European mainland late in the eighth century to distinguish the Saxons who lived in England from those who lived on the continent. These invaders were the first of the purely Germanic peoples to settle in Britain.

Their homes had lain outside the Roman empire and they were almost untouched by Mediterranean civilisation. They were illiterate except for a knowledge of runes which had a very limited application, and they worshipped heathen gods of whom very little is known. They were uncivilised, in the sense that a Roman citizen might have interpreted this term, and they buried their dead either by cremation or by inhumation in shallow graves, generally without raising mounds above them.

It is well that the illiteracy of the invaders should be stressed, so that there may be the less danger of interpreting at their face value the scanty English records which profess to relate the progress of the invasions. Two hundred years were to pass before even a small number of the English learnt to read, and still longer before they began to write down the little that was remembered about their earliest days in Britain. There are, apart from the written English traditions and some documents of Welsh and Gaulish origin, two principal means of determining the extent of land occupied by the English during the fifth and sixth centuries: first, the study of relics recovered from burials, that is to say the pottery, the jewellery worn by the women and the arms carried by the men; and second, the study of the names which the invaders gave to the places where they lived. It is difficult, and perhaps impossible, to establish an accurate chronology from material of this kind, but it may be believed that the most easily accessible parts of the country had been deeply penetrated before 500 A.D.

There is not enough evidence to determine how the invasions were carried out, whether piecemeal or with some degree of organisation, but it is certain that they were wholly unlike the highly organised military undertakings of the Romans in 43 A.D. and the Normans in 1066. The English aimed at colonisation, not merely the imposition of military rule upon a conquered country. English tradition represents the first invaders as coming in small groups of two or three shiploads at a time, and doubtless this often occurred, but it seems no less probable that an undertaking so vast in scope and so successful in outcome would sometimes demand more than mere piecemeal nibbling. In the south-east of Britain where the country was most exposed to attack, the British seem to have been overwhelmed in the first onslaught. Yet even here they were able to achieve a temporary recovery which not only halted the English advance, but may even have led to the return of some of the invaders to the continent. In the north, however, penetration of the highland zone was a much more difficult task, and here the British seem to have maintained their ascendancy until the beginning of the seventh century. In this northern zone the invasions scarcely amounted to more than the imposition of an English aristocracy, and of course the English language, upon a predominantly Celtic civilisation.

It is no more possible to say exactly when the invasions came to an end than it is to say precisely when they began, but if a date is needed to mark the transition from the first to the second phase within these six centuries, the year 597 is perhaps the most suitable. This was the year in which Augustine landed in Thanet at the head of a mission from Rome, which led to the conversion of the reigning king of Kent and to the renewal of contact with Mediterranean civilisation. For about two hundred years after this event, while medieval Europe was beginning to take shape, and before the Viking storm broke, England enjoyed one of the rare periods in her history of freedom from both the reality and the threat of external attack; and in that freedom there was opportunity for a new civilisation to develop. Roman rule had imposed a unity upon the greater part of Britain, a unity which was lost in fact for a time, but it may yet have remained in a tradition which was not wholly without its effect upon the newcomers (see p. 90).

When written historical records first become trustworthy, in the seventh century, it is possible to discern about a dozen English states. Some are like Kent and Sussex whose boundaries coincided closely with those of the modern counties, others like Mercia and Northumbria embracing much wider territories; and all were governed by kings. The political history of the seventh and eighth centuries consists largely of the gradual elimination of the smaller states as independent kingdoms and the consolidation and expansion of the larger ones, a process which marked an important stage in the achievement of a unity more real than any that had been imposed by Rome. Northumbria was dominant in the seventh century and her kings, who can be recognised as belonging to the passing Teutonic Heroic Age, steadily advanced the frontiers of English territory westwards to the Irish Sea and northwards to Edinburgh and the Firth of Forth. The medieval world comes much nearer in the eighth century in which the most significant fact of English political history is that two kings between them ruled in Mercia for some eighty years and in their long reigns they achieved for the block of midland territory, which lies between Thames and Humber, a predominance which kept their northern and southern neighbours politically in the background. Æthelbald, the earlier of these two Mercian rulers, is the first English king to whom the title *rex Brittaniae* is known to have been applied. Offa, the second, was not only the builder of the great dyke which defined the border between England and Wales virtually where it runs to-day, but he was also a man of sufficient prominence in Europe to be treated with respect by the pope and to feel himself entitled to deal on equal terms with Charlemagne. The last stage in the political unification of England is marked by another southerly shift of power with the emergence of the great rulers of Wessex, but this belongs to the period after the Viking attacks had begun.

Apart from such a man as Offa, the English kings of this intermediate phase often seem to be little more than petty princelings of no great significance, even though there were scholars among them. Yet the great treasure, which was found at Sutton Hoo near Ipswich in 1939, has forcibly revealed that a provincial king (if such the owner was), whose territory embraced scarcely more than two modern English counties, might yet be a man of very considerable wealth derived from every quarter of the western world. It seems yet uncertain whether the ship in which he was buried was bound for the realms of the heathen gods or for the Christian heaven, but whichever it was, he took with him a great share of this world's goods. Among them were a dozen pieces of silver plate, including a magnificent silver dish which had been made in the Byzantine empire during the reign of Anastasius I (491–518), and was therefore already an antique when it was placed in the ship near the middle of the seventh century. The other silver pieces likewise belong to the Mediterranean world rather than to the Germanic north. From the latter, and perhaps in particular from Sweden, came his shield and helmet, both of them badly crushed and broken when the roof of the burial chamber collapsed, but now restored, if only to a rather pale reflection of their original splendour. The crown of the helmet had been decorated with a gilded crest and with embossed panels of bronze representing now forgotten episodes of the Heroic Age, and the remarkable vizor gleamed with garnets and threads of inlaid silver wire. From Merovingian France came forty gold coins, and from England itself, surpassing all the rest both in beauty and technical excellence, came jewellery wrought of gold, garnets and coloured glass (see Plate 22).

This great treasure from Sutton Hoo, now preserved in the British Museum, is a legacy from the topmost layer of early English society, the royal families. Closely associated with them were the nobility and the higher officers of the church. At the other end of the scale there was a considerable slave population, but little is heard of them except by indirect reference, since they had no rights according to the law of the times. Between the two came the mass of what may be called the English people, the people whose achievements can be traced in broad outline, but whose individual voices can never be heard, unless perhaps in the riddles which formed part of their entertainment.

If anyone were to maintain that the greatest and most enduring achievement of the English people in the whole period of their history between 450 and 1066 was the achievement which changed the face of great stretches of the countryside, which cleared uncounted thousands of acres of forest, which established innumerable villages, farms and tracks across the length and breadth of the country, it might be difficult to deny that he was right. But this achievement is one of which the records give little direct information. Here there is a reference to the open field system of agriculture in Wessex, and there a glimpse of small villages scattered about the north, with sheep playing a large part in their economy. Much of the story may yet be recovered from studying the charters which record the boundaries of estates and the names not only of villages and hamlets, but even of the fields which surround them. The appearance of many of these fields has been changed by the hedgerow, although there were large areas of the country which never knew the open field system of agriculture. It would, of course, be a mistake to suppose that this process of clearing was completed within the Anglo-Saxon period, but it was certainly greatly advanced.

Primarily, then, this early English society was a farming society with the village, hamlet or farm as its units, and with corn-growing or cattle-raising as its main activities. The Englishman of the time was not a town-dweller. Some towns there were, including London, Canterbury and York, but all the English towns, whose existence can be established before the Viking attacks began, were on Roman sites, and several of them were also the seats of bishops (see p. 100). This is no argument for the continuity of town life from Roman times, since many of the towns of Roman Britain had fallen into decay before the Romans left; but there is evidence here and there, from such places as Canterbury in the south and Carlisle in the north, which may suggest such continuity.

The use of Roman sites as episcopal seats is perhaps more significant, and it may well be that the beginnings of English town life were partly due to the reoccupation of the Roman towns as administrative centres for the Roman church. But even if this early England is regarded primarily as an agricultural and pastoral country, it ought not to be supposed that it had no internal or foreign trade. Penny, shilling and pound are all terms which were current in England long before the Norman Conquest, and the silver coinage which was issued by Offa in the eighth century was of such excellence that it survived without any major reform until the time of Henry II. Moreover Offa thought it worth while to issue a gold coinage which would be an acceptable medium of currency to Arab traders, and the closure of the continental markets to English merchants because of a quarrel between Offa and Charlemagne is a measure of the trade which was then passing between England and the mainland.

The church played a leading part in establishing and maintaining these foreign contacts. Any discussion of Christianity in Britain before the English invasion would be inappropriate here, but the early history of the English church is not to be understood without a realisation that the Britain which the English invaded was already largely, and perhaps predominantly, Christian. The conversion of the English, which began with Kent in 597, was, nominally at least, completed during the seventh century. Soon after Augustine reached England he wrote to Gregory in Rome to ask his advice on the many difficult problems which faced him in his task. Not least among these problems were those which concerned the attitude he was to adopt on the one hand towards English heathenism and on the other towards the clergy of the British church. On the first point he was finally advised not to be too rigorous, but to adopt a policy of conciliation by establishing as much continuity with the old ways as was consistent with Christian belief. And on the second, he was bluntly told that he was to regard all the British clergy as being under his care. It mattered little that Gregory's paper scheme for the organisation of the English church, with metropolitans at London and York and twelve suffragans under each, was wholly remote from reality. Organisation would grow in time. But this ill-conceived attitude towards the Celtic church was a matter of much greater seriousness.

It is difficult to estimate the respective parts played in the conversion of the English by Roman and Celtic missionaries, but there is no doubt that the missionary spirit was strong in the Celtic church, particularly in its Irish or Scottish branch. Celtic missionaries were active in Mercia, Essex and East Anglia, as well as in Northumbria. And it was here, in Northumbria, that the conflict between the two churches came to a head. One of the results of the English invasion of Britain had been to isolate this western Celtic church from Rome, and as it grew and prospered vigorously in its isolation, it was bound to diverge along paths of its own. The wonder is that in its hundred and fifty years of isolation it had come to diverge only in its outward forms and not in its theology as well. Superficially the matters in dispute at the famous synod which was held at Whitby in about 664 were matters of outward form: the right way of calculating the date of Easter, the ritual to be observed in baptism, the form of the tonsure and so forth. But the fundamental issue was of far greater importance than any of these outward forms. It was the decision whether the Christian community in

England was to recognise the authority of the pope in Rome as its head and so to become a part of the Roman Catholic church, or whether it was to establish itself as a wholly independent Christian community on the extreme western fringe of the known world. There were parts of the Celtic church which had already made their decision in favour of Rome, and the vigorous leadership of Wilfrid won the day for the Roman party at Whitby. The church in England became, as it was to remain until the Reformation, part of the church of Rome.

Soon after the synod of Whitby a fortunate chance brought to Canterbury a man of outstanding ability, Theodore of Tarsus, and to him was given the task of removing the weaknesses which had been left by the conflict and of introducing regular diocesan organisation. The results of his work are reflected partly in that remarkable and sometimes neglected achievement of the English church in the eighth century, the English mission to the continental Saxons and their neighbours, a valiant and successful attempt to bring Christianity to the heathen people whom they knew to be their own ancestors. It is reflected even more splendidly in the great achievements of this new and united church, part English, part Mediterranean and part Celtic, which placed England, and particularly Northumbria (represented primarily in the person of Bede), in the forefront of European civilisation.

The Christian church, whether it came from the Celtic north and west, from Gaul or from Rome, brought with it the knowledge of reading and writing, the seeds from which English scholarship rose to great heights in the eighth century. Modern England has inherited a rich legacy of books, illuminated manuscripts and sculptured stones from this period. At the head stands Bede's *Ecclesiastical History of the English Nation* which can still be read in a manuscript written in 737, only two years after Bede's death, which now forms one of the most precious treasures of Cambridge University Library. This manuscript, which is almost completely free from even the simplest forms of ornament, offers what is perhaps the nearest approach which can now be made to the person of Bede himself. For contrast there is the magnificent splendour of the Lindisfarne Gospels, a book, now preserved in the British Museum, which welds the products of three civilisations into a single incomparable whole (see Plate 23). For its text is used the Vulgate which had first been brought from Rome to England by Augustine. Some also of its decoration, particularly the full page drawings of the Evangelists, was likewise derived from Mediterranean sources. The Northumbrian artists of these times were ill at ease in their attempts to portray the human figure, but in their abstract designs, in which Celtic linear motifs were used alongside animal and bird patterns from the Germanic world, they achieved a turbulent brilliance which has seldom been equalled. Rivalling the painters were the sculptors, whose work is still to be seen in scores of parish churches, or occasionally, like the great cross-shaft at Bewcastle, standing outside in the churchyard. The sculptors were more successful than the painters in portraying the human figure, but their greatest achievements lay in elaborate interlace patterns and in the vine-scroll with birds and beasts pecking at bunches of grapes.

Alongside this art of manuscript and sculptured cross, alongside the Latin literature of Bede and Aldhelm, there is found another phenomenon which, like the crosses, is without parallel in western Europe at this time: the development of a literature, both secular and ecclesiastical, and written not in Latin but in the vernacular English, or Old English as philologists call it. From Kent there is a code of laws which was written about 600 A.D. and is by far the earliest surviving body of Germanic law written in the vernacular. English also came to be used for charters and for the annalistic form of historical record, the foundation of the great work now known as the Anglo-Saxon Chronicle. But above all it was used for the transmission of the native alliterative verse. Much of this verse, which was a literature both of entertainment and of instruction, was composed for recitation, perhaps to the accompaniment of a harp such as was found at Sutton Hoo, and was of a religious kind. Some of it, however, was in the elegiac mood, and in its treatment of timeless themes of universal application it still endures comparison with the poetry of any age. Such were *The Seafarer, The Wanderer, The Ruin, The Wife's Lament,* titles which suggest the nature of their content clearly enough. These short elegies are overshadowed by the great epic poem *Beowulf* now preserved in a West Saxon English version of the tenth century, but belonging to a much earlier age. In its kind it is a legacy no less precious than Bede's *History,* the Lindisfarne Gospels or the Bewcastle Cross.

Bede did not carry his History beyond 731 A.D. and he himself died four years later. For more than a century after his death the records of English history are everywhere scanty, a fact which may in part be ascribed to the Viking attacks, which began near the end of the eighth century and mark the transition to the third phase of Anglo-Saxon history. Even though Bede had observed signs of decay and abuse in Northumbrian monasticism, there is evidence enough to indicate that high levels of scholarship were maintained for many years after his death, particularly in York, which came to surpass Monkwearmouth and Jarrow as the most important centre of English learning in the eighth century.

Within a few years of 800 A.D. contemporary annalists recorded three seaborne attacks against various parts of the British Isles; one against Lindisfarne where Cuthbert had been a monk, one against Iona whence Aidan had come to preach Christianity to Northumbria some ten years after the Roman mission led by Paulinus, and one against the south coast of Wessex near Portland. These attacks marked the beginning of a process which worked profound changes in every aspect of English life, and indeed there was no country of western Europe which remained unaffected. The causes of this new movement of peoples, scarcely less great in extent than the earlier migrations which had first brought the English to Britain, seem to have been partly economic and partly political, but the defencelessness of western Europe was in no small degree responsible for the development of freebooting piracy into large-scale migration. When Alcuin first heard of the sack of Lindisfarne he wrote expressing his astonishment at the mere possibility of such an event befalling. Had there been even the least suspicion that danger might come across the seas, Lindisfarne would have been almost the last place to choose for a monastic community. But scattered around the coasts of western Europe were many other religious communities on sites which, like Lindisfarne, had been chosen for the very reason that they seemed to offer the greatest security from external interference. There was wealth here for the taking, as the bent and broken pieces of reliquaries and book bindings in Scandinavian museums still testify. While the Swedes moved mainly towards the east and quickly penetrated as far as Constantinople, Danes and Norwegians turned towards the west and south, embracing Britain in the two arms of their attack, which on the one side reached south through the Narrow Seas and along the Channel, and on the other west to the Faroes, Shetland, Orkney, the Western Isles and Ireland. In the earliest stages there seems to have been no thought of colonisation. The raiders came with the easterly winds of spring and returned with their booty the same year. The frequency of attack grew steadily and by the middle of the ninth century the Vikings had begun to pass the winter in England, establishing themselves near coastal bases such as Thanet or Sheppey could supply, but even then they remained in England only that they might start campaigning so much the earlier when spring came. It was not until 865 A.D., when the Great Army, as men called it, landed on the shores of East Anglia, that raiding gave way to conquest and permanent settlement.

Opinions about the Vikings are still largely coloured by the views of monastic writers, one of whom called them 'this furious, ferocious, ruthless, wrathful, pagan people'. And certainly they were in some respects a barbaric people who destroyed many centres of learning with all their records. York, which had boasted one of the greatest libraries of western Europe in the eighth century, became instead the capital of a line of pagan kings, culminating in Eric Bloodaxe, the husband of a notorious witch. It was a long time before the archbishopric recovered. Yet it would be a great mistake to regard these newcomers to England as no more than heathen pirates, and to forget that their misdeeds are recorded mainly by those who suffered most at their hands. Even though the ferocity of their world is not to be denied, theirs was a world also of great enchantment peopled by Thor who disguised himself as a bride to recover his hammer, by Othin who rode his eight-legged horse followed by his two ravens, by Baldr whom none but the mistletoe could slay and by Heimdalr who sat by the rainbow's end ready to blow his great trumpet when Ragnarökr should come, his ears so sharp that he could hear the wool growing upon a sheep's back. Their mythology is full of a lively humour which often shows slight respect for the gods themselves, and in the art of story-telling they have seldom been surpassed. Their love of intricate and complex design, which is revealed in their woodcarving and metalwork, recurs in their literature, especially in their verse. They had, and many of their descendants still have, a remarkable facility for composing lampoons, usually blunt and much to the point. But for centuries this literature was wholly oral, and it is a measure of the differing levels of civilisation that, whereas the English had developed a flourishing written literature by the eighth century, no historical or literary work composed by a native of Scandinavia was put into writing until more than four hundred years later.

The landing of the Great Army in 865 A.D. led swiftly to the complete disruption of the existing political organisation of England. For ten years it campaigned almost unchecked up and down the country, moving from place to place on horseback, but fighting on foot. Of the four kingdoms whose position had been consolidated during the two previous centuries, three—Northumbria, Mercia and East Anglia —ceased to exist as independent units. Northumbria, still stretching far north across the lowlands of Scotland, was truncated in the south by the loss of Yorkshire. The eastern half of Mercia and the whole of East Anglia were settled by disbanded viking armies, and came to form part of the territory known as the Danelaw, that is to say the lands in which Danish law or custom prevailed. Wessex alone survived under the leadership of Alfred, who was able to organise resistance from within the security of the Somerset marshes beyond Selwood, and to start the slow and steady process of reconquest which was the great glory of the Wessex kings. The destruction of the other English kingdoms in the ninth century, and the reconquest of the Danelaw by the kings of Wessex in the tenth, marked the final stage in the establishment of England as a single political unit under monarchical government, although the succession was to be broken more than once by new conquerors. At one stage Alfred had lost control of almost all his lands, yet Æthelstan, his grandson, had every right to call himself king of England. The border with Wales had long since been established, and in the tenth century the border with Scotland began to take shape, as the kingdom of Scotland itself emerged from the union of the Pictish and Scottish crowns, and absorbed most of the English and British territories which lay between the two old Roman frontiers.

Although the political unity of England was established, a very large part of the country had become

K

Scandinavian in race, language and custom, with Danes predominating in the east, and a not inconsiderable Norse population, approaching by way of the Western Isles and Ireland, establishing themselves in the north-west. In short, the ninth and tenth centuries saw a fresh colonisation which was no less important and hardly less extensive than the English settlements themselves. Place-names alone tell the story vividly enough, but much else of modern England came into being at this time.

It is a curious circumstance that, despite their love of fighting, the Vikings had a great respect for law and considerable ability as administrators and organisers. One of the greatest of the Icelandic sagas is largely woven round this honouring of the law, and no one who has studied the history of Iceland in the tenth and eleventh centuries need find himself surprised by the efficiency of Norman rule in England. It is fundamental to modern English conceptions of government that the votes of a majority should be binding on all concerned, but the operation of this principal in England is first to be observed in a code of laws which relates to part of the Danelaw. An enquiry into the administrative boundaries of modern England, both civil and ecclesiastical, would show that the great majority of them first become recognisable in the two centuries which separate the Danish invasions from the Norman Conquest. Some may be older, though none so old as the Roman period. The shires of Wessex are probably the oldest of the English counties, apart from those which had once been independent kingdoms, but with the exception of the northern group, all the rest were in existence before the middle of the eleventh century, though naturally it is not to be supposed that their boundaries have invariably remained unchanged ever since. The counties of the midlands are much more regular and artificial in appearance than are the Wessex shires, and there is some ground for thinking that, more particularly in the east midlands, they owe their origin in part to the methods adopted by the Danish armies for the division of conquered territory among their number, and in part to the system of military organisation applied by Alfred in Wessex and later by Edward the Elder in the midlands.

Alderman and sheriff are two twentieth-century terms of local government which are found in the records of the tenth and the eleventh centuries, though both have undergone many changes of meaning in the course of the intervening centuries. These terms are both of English origin; so also are *shire* (though not *county* which is Norman-French), *hundred*, *rape* and *lathe*, all of which were functioning in their various localities in the tenth century and some of them much earlier, but the *wapentakes* of the north-eastern midlands and the *ridings* of Lindsey and Yorkshire are Scandinavian. Riding is derived from an Old Norse word meaning 'a third part' and other ridings are to be found in Orkney, Norway, Sweden and even as far away as the island of Gotland in the Baltic. Closely connected with the administration of both hundred and wapentake was a council of twelve men of the neighbourhood, an institution which came to play a very important part in the history of these and later times, and was almost certainly introduced from Scandinavia. There is a sense in which such a council can be called a jury, but that sense is very remote from the modern meaning of this term. Where so much of terminology and even of function survived in matters of local government into modern times, it is significant that the Old English *witenagemot*, the meeting of the king's councillors, has perished and that parliament, another Norman-French importation, has taken its place.

In its social organisation the Scandinavian world did not differ fundamentally from the English, since both had inherited much from a common Germanic background. The changes which English society underwent in the tenth and eleventh centuries arose rather from changing economic conditions than from the introduction of new social conceptions from Scandinavia. The need experienced by both English and Danes alike for some kind of defensible centre was among the factors which stimulated the growth of town life at this period. In several areas these fortified centres have developed into the county towns of to-day, such for example as Bedford, Huntingdon and Northampton, or further north, Nottingham and Derby. A system which had been devised to provide greater security in times of invasion provided also the means of establishing greater control over internal trade. The buying and selling of merchandise and the coining of money were confined by law to these centres, both to the profit of the king and to the advantage of the merchants who gained a market for their goods. London had already been a mercantile centre of some importance in the time of Bede. In the first half of the tenth century eight moneyers were employed there, and at the end of the century the wharves of Billingsgate were receiving a rich variety of cargoes from France and the Low Countries.

There is no evidence that the Scandinavian invaders brought with them any major innovations in farming practice, but the long periods of warfare led to great changes in the structure of rural society. Alfred had found difficulty in keeping his armies in the field at harvest time, and the loss of a harvest must often have resulted in a farmer losing his independence. The plight of the English farming community went steadily from bad to worse during the tenth and eleventh centuries, until the economic status of the individual farmer had come near to that of the medieval villein over large areas of the countryside. The economic depression of the small farmer was accompanied by the formation of great estates, whose holders were occasionally powerful enough to challenge the authority of the lawful government. In this way, with the weak needing the protection of the strong, the seeds of feudalism were being sown. But on the other side of the boundary, within the Danelaw, the rank and file of the disbanded Danish armies possessed themselves of lands in a freedom from ties of service and lordship, which they were able to maintain for many generations.

The organisation of the church was seriously disrupted by the Viking invasions, particularly in the northern and eastern parts of the country, and monastic life seems almost to have ceased. Lindisfarne, Jarrow, Hartlepool and Whitby were among the many monastic houses which were destroyed, yet it is easy to exaggerate the destructive effects of the kind of warfare from which the country suffered at various times between 865 A.D. and 1066. Armies were small and much of their destruction was of a kind which could quickly be made good. In time many of the settlers became Christians, like the warrior whose memorial stands at Nunburnholme in Yorkshire (see Plate 24), and bears upon one of its faces a crude representation of the Madonna and Child.

Moreover there were large areas which were scarcely touched, and it was from one such, western Mercia, that there came to Alfred's court a distinguished group of scholars to help him in his literary and educational work. In 878 this remarkable man had little left but an island fortress in the Somerset marshes, but ten years later, then a man rising forty, he ruled a wide kingdom and was learning Latin, so that he could make those translations of ancient books which can now be recognised as the foundations of English prose literature. It was a very sound instinct which bestowed on this man alone of all the kings of England the title of The Great.

Alfred's attempts to re-establish monastic life met with only small success, but with the return of momentarily more settled times in the latter part of the tenth century there began, at first independently and later under strong influence from reformed continental centres, that great revival of Benedictine monasticism which is associated with such men as Dunstan, Æthelwold and Oswald and with such places as Glastonbury, Worcester and Winchester in the south and Ramsey, Ely and Peterborough in the east. The building of churches and the writing of service books were among the most enduring outward signs of this reborn monasticism. The Rhineland was the source of many of the architectural features of the churches of this period whose remains are to be seen in the monastic church at Deerhurst, the little chapel of St. Lawrence at Bradford-on-Avon, the great tower at Earl's Barton in Northamptonshire, perhaps the most impressive architectural monument of the Anglo-Saxon period, and the tower at Sompting in Sussex and also many other parish churches. The Rhineland too gave inspiration for the new styles of decorative art which are to be seen in the foundation charter of the New Minster at Winchester, now in the British Museum, or in the great Benedictional of Æthelwold, now at Chatsworth. No less important in its contribution to medieval English civilisation was the growth of a new literature, which was mainly religious in character and did much towards the further development of the English language as an adaptable vehicle of narrative prose.

Setting aside the Industrial Revolution and the world of modern science, there is scarcely any aspect of English life to-day which has not inherited something from these six hundred years of English history, and each may well have his own opinion on what is the most valuable part of this great legacy. Some may turn towards the field of government, observing the gradual political unification of England under a largely hereditary monarchy, and the establishment of a machinery of local government needing only the strong hand of Norman rule to extract from it the full efficiency of which it was capable. Others may turn towards the countryside, noting the growth of market towns and the laborious creation of arable and pasture out of scrub and forest, a labour whose results are still being enjoyed by English farmers to-day. Yet others may cherish the works of literature and learning, particularly of those authors whose attachment to their own language prepared the ground for the achievements of later times. But there will certainly be some who will value most highly the long tradition of Christian civilisation inherited from Augustine and Canterbury, Cuthbert and Holy Island, Bede and Jarrow, Dunstan and Glastonbury—the once living men and the still living places.

SUGGESTIONS FOR FURTHER READING

F. M. Stenton, *Anglo-Saxon England*, 1943, 2nd ed. 1947.

R. H. Hodgkin, *A History of the Anglo-Saxons*, 1935, 2nd ed. 1939.

R. Jessup, *Anglo-Saxon Jewellery*, 1950.

T D. Kendrick, *Anglo-Saxon Art to* A.D. 900, 1938.

T. D. Kendrick, *Late Saxon and Viking Art*, 1949.

G. K. Anderson, *The Literature of the Anglo-Saxons*, Princeton, 1949.

C. W. Kennedy, *The Earliest English Poetry*, 1943.

E. S. Duckett, *Anglo-Saxon Saints and Scholars*, New York, 1947.

VII

EDWARD MILLER

The Norman Conquest

I

ON January 5th, 1066, Edward the Confessor died,
leaving no direct heir to succeed him. Next
day Harold of Wessex, the most powerful man in
England, was crowned at Westminster in his place.
Harold must already have known that his elevation
would not pass uncontested. William, Duke of
Normandy, had long coveted the English crown.
Fifteen years earlier the Confessor may even have
promised that he should succeed. Later, Harold
himself had been tricked into swearing an oath to
further Duke William's interests. Harold's accession,
however, meant that if William wanted the English
throne he would have to fight for it. This he determined to do, though not a few of his Norman vassals
'were opposed to so difficult an undertaking, and
alleged that a handful of Normans were unequal to
conquering the numerous hosts of the English.'

His decision taken, William acted with astonishing
speed. Allies were gained and troops recruited from
far outside the borders of Normandy. The Pope's
blessing was won by William's diplomats. A fleet was
built, an invasion force concentrated in the Channel
ports, and by early September all was ready. In face

of these preparations King Harold had not been idle. He had gathered a fleet in the Channel and set strong garrisons all along the south coast. But the wind blew consistently up the Channel and William could not move. This delay was too much for the rudimentary services of the English fighting forces in the eleventh century; and Harold was compelled to disband much of his fleet and army as supplies ran out. It was just at this moment that news came to the king of another invasion in the north. His own outlawed brother, Tostig, and King Harold Hardrada of Norway had landed in Yorkshire and had defeated the armies of north and midland England at Fulford. So Harold had to set out, by forced marches, for the north; there, on September 25th, he practically annihilated the Scandanavian forces at the battle of Stamford Bridge. Meantime, the wind had changed. What followed may be set down in the words of an Anglo-Saxon chronicler:—

Then came William count of Normandy to Pevensey on St. Michael's mass-eve [Sept. 28th]; and immediately after they were ready they constructed a castle at the town of Hastings. This was then made known to king Harold, and he gathered a great army, and he came to meet him at the hoar apple-tree. And William came against him unawares, ere his people were in battle order. But the king, nevertheless, boldly fought against him with those men who would follow him; and there was a great slaughter made on either side. There were slain king Harold, and earl Leofwine his brother, and earl Gyrth his brother, and many good men; and the French had possession of the place of carnage, as to them God granted for the people's sins.

The Norman victory at Hastings, on Saturday October 14th, 1066, was only the beginning of the Conquest; but it was a decisive victory. The combined losses of the battles of Fulford, Stamford Bridge and Hastings had seriously reduced Saxon military resources. The death of Harold and many other great men greatly impaired any capacity for co-ordinated resistance. By Christmas William had occupied London. On Christmas Day the Archbishop of York 'hallowed him to king' in Westminster Abbey. After that it was a matter of crushing in detail the remaining pockets of resistance. For five years English risings continued and had to be put down. Exeter defied William in 1067; there were risings in Somerset and Dorset, and under Edric the Wild in Hereford; the north had to be twice conquered; and Hereward made the Isle of Ely 'a camp of refuge' for English dissidents from all over the country from the summer of 1070 until well into 1071. Some of these revolts were severe tests for William's precarious hold on England, but they were surmounted. By 1075, danger was coming rather from rebellion amongst his own followers; and Englishmen fought in the army which put down the rising of the earls. In 1079 a Saxon, Topi the son of Wigot of Wallingford, was to save William's life at the siege of Gerberoi.

Such are the bare facts about the Norman Conquest. The changes which followed, however, were decisive for much of later English history, even if not quite so catastrophic as has sometimes been supposed. The English who won at Stamford Bridge and lost at Hastings were, we know, not quite as Milton pictured them: 'The great men given to gluttony and dissolute life, . . . the meaner sort tippling together night and day . . . attended with other vices which effeminate men's minds'. But neither were the Normans who conquered them mere robber barons. They were, moreover, the last of the conquerors of these islands. Immigrants have continued to come to Britain since 1066—French, Flemish and Jewish immigrants; and they have made important contributions to our national life. But they have come as individuals, in small groups, as refugees. The followers of William the Conqueror were the last of the many invaders of Britain who had it in their power to divert the main stream of national development, and to add an important strain to the mongrel blood of Englishmen. They were the last people from beyond the narrow seas to contribute to the heritage of early Britain.

II

In order to understand the Norman contribution, we must begin with the character of their settlement on English soil. In this particular, it is not altogether irrelevant to notice that the new settlers were not by any means all Normans. The very army which won the battle of Hastings had a Breton contingent on its left flank and a French contingent on the right, as well as Norman knights in the place of honour in the centre. This diversity continued into the period of settlement. The Domesday survey, which William ordered to be made in 1086, provides a directory of the more important of the settlers. The majority, it is true, were Norman lords; but there was a notable contingent from Brittany and a fair number of other men from elsewhere in France—from the Boulonais, Picardy and Flanders. This diversity of origin is important:

it established links between England and parts of western Europe other than Normandy alone, and brought other than merely Norman influences to bear upon post-Conquest England.

It is equally important not to overemphasise the number of settlers. Precisely how many of them there were no one can accurately determine, but William's army at Hastings was probably not much more than five thousand strong. Of this number many were killed, and some of them went home again after the battle was over. On the other hand, of course, others came over to England to seek their fortune there once victory was achieved. By 1086 there may have been some five or six thousand foreign knights in England— most of them tenants or followers of a few hundred lay or ecclesiastical magnates who were also generally foreigners by that date. There were certainly other 'Normans' too: royal servants and technicians like Nigel the Doctor, Bernard the Falconer, Waleran the Hunter and Odard the Crossbowman; some clerks and priests and monks; and some men of the trading classes like the French burgesses of Norwich, Nottingham and Northampton. We cannot add these numbers up; perhaps they amounted to somewhere between six and ten thousand men. No doubt many of these men ultimately brought over wives and families, although other Normans, like the members of all armies of occupation, found wives from the womenfolk of the conquered people. It may, however, put the scale of the settlement into proportion if we realise that the total population of England at the time probably amounted to between one and two million people.

There is another significant fact. The Norman

settlers did not (like the Jutes and the Danes earlier on) cling together in a limited territory. Indeed, to call them settlers in the first generation may almost convey a false impression. They were rather an army of occupation, holding England down from the castles they built everywhere at strategic points in the wake of the armies of conquest. The settlers, therefore, were not only few; they were also thinly spread. In the long run this must have favoured their assimilation. In the short run, both factors limited the extent of the Conquest. Ireland was not touched in the early days; the independence of the Welsh principalities was substantially unimpaired; and Scotland included a good deal of what we regard as England. The Tweed might mark the beginning of Scotland in the east, though the Tyne was really the end of England. In the west, on the other hand, something like the modern boundary was only created by William Rufus. In the Conqueror's day the Scottish dominion came down to Rere Cross on Stainmore, only two days ride from York. In the centuries which followed, there was much Anglo-Norman expansion into the Celtic west, but the initial limitations of the Norman Conquest did something to preserve the individuality of the Celtic lands. Even in England, furthermore, the thin layer of Norman settlement was never weighty enough to crush out of existence strongly marked provincial differences inherited from Old English times. If those differences are less marked than they used to be, that is a consequence of the development of mass communications in far more modern times.

The slightness, the thinness, the very military character of the Norman settlement at first, therefore, had important consequences of a negative sort. They explain the real continuity between Saxon and Norman England, and the preservation down to later times of elements of the Old English heritage. The Norman army of occupation in many respects simply took over a going concern. They used it for their own purposes, but they changed it relatively little. They took over the economic assets of Saxon England; English land continued to be tilled by Saxon and Danish peasants in the traditional way, even though the owners of the land were new. They took over much of the administrative system of Saxon times, and above all the shire and its courts and its officers. The Conqueror was also anxious to stress the fact that he was the rightful successor of Edward the Confessor, and therefore heir to the material and moral assets won for the royal office by the house of Alfred the Great. Even the English language survived in the long run. It ceased for a time to be the language of literature, where it was replaced by Latin. It ceased to be the language of the upper classes, who spoke French. It was banished to the humbler homes of peasants and townsmen; but it emerged eventually, with a Romance infusion no doubt, as the language of all. Long before that happened, however, the old distinction between Norman and Saxon had been obliterated. Indeed, a civil servant could say, little more than a century after the Conquest:

Nowadays, when English and Normans . . . marry and give in marriage to each other, the nations are so mixed that it can scarcely be decided . . . who is of English and who of Norman birth.

By that date, what we may properly call English history had begun.

III

Yet, if there was continuity across 'the red thread of the Norman Conquest', there was also change and novelty after 1066. In the first place attention may be drawn to the ties with Europe which the Conquest established. Such ties, we know, were not new; for these studies of the heritage of early Britain have been much concerned with them. England has never in any real sense been cut off from influences flowing across the Channel from the main centres of continental civilisation. But the Conquest could not but give these connections a greater intimacy. The Conqueror's dominions bridged the Channel. Many of his greatest subjects had lands and kinsfolk on both sides of the narrow seas. Less than a century after the battle of Hastings, the accession of Henry II of Anjou to the English throne brought under a common rule territories stretching from the Tweed and the Solway to the shores of the Mediterranean. True, most of these territories were lost to the kings of France by the early thirteenth century; but for some generations after 1066 England was part of western Europe in a far more real sense than at any time since the ending of the Roman occupation. Furthermore, these links were forged precisely at the time when the characteristically medieval civilisation was taking shape in Europe. Political order was being restored after the chaos of the Dark Ages. An economic revival was taking place. The Papacy was reforming and uniting the western church. An intellectual renaissance was beginning, which drew not only upon its own resources but also upon the legacy of classical civilisation and the learning of the Islamic peoples. The Europe to which the Normans united England was a Europe from which England had very much to learn.

In this connection, however, we may hardly pass over the harsh judgement upon the Normans with which Sir Frank Stenton ends his great book on Anglo-Saxon England:

> The Normans who entered into the English inheritance (he writes) were a harsh and violent race. They were the closest of all the western peoples to the barbarian strain in the western order. They had produced little in art or learning, and nothing in literature, that could be set beside the work of Englishmen.

Such a people might bring to England the military arts of their day—the arts of castle-building and of fighting on horseback. They are less likely to have been carriers of the arts of peace. That is perhaps true even despite the revolution they made in English ecclesiastical architecture. The first generation after the Conquest was a time of intense building activity, a time (in Bishop Wulfstan's words) when 'destroying the works of our forefathers, we laboured to heap up stones'. The predominant influence in all this activity was certainly a Norman influence, the influence of the Norman variety of the Romanesque style. Though much has gone, the effect of this influence is still visible in our churches. The remains of Norman building—at Ely, at Winchester, at St. John's Chapel in the Tower—are often plain and even crude. They also have their own harsh magnificence, and they did provide the point of departure for the development of medieval church architecture in England.

In a consideration of this aspect of Norman influence, however, there is something more to be said. The

L

Normans claimed no monopoly in the use of the bridge they built across the Channel. Even our medieval churches are witness to this fact. The buildings at Hereford and Old Sarum from the first generation after 1066 display influences which seem to have come from the Rhineland. Later, Cistercian monks brought incipient Gothic tendencies from Burgundy to remote valleys in Yorkshire and Lancashire. Only the stone of Canterbury Cathedral choir came from Normandy. Its first architect came from Sens in central France; and it was finished by an Englishman after his predecessor had fallen fifty feet from the scaffolding and, 'finding no benefit from the skill of surgeons, went to France to die at home'.

What is true of church-building is also true of other things. For long after the first settlement of the Normans, there was a steady trickle of men from many parts of Europe bringing with them to England the knowledge and the experience of the European renaissance. It is characteristic enough that the first two Norman Archbishops of Canterbury, Lanfranc and St. Anselm, were both Italians and both men of European reputation. They helped to introduce into the English church new views about ecclesiastical reform and some of the new learning of the continental schools. Bishop Roger of Salisbury, too, a great civil servant in the days of Henry I, was said to have been picked up by that king at a wayside church in his French dominions. The virtue which commended him was the capacity to say Mass more rapidly than most men. In the following reign, an Italian was teaching Roman law at Canterbury, and he may even have taught at Oxford. Even in the thirteenth century Simon de Montfort, once described, for his services to

English liberties, as 'that buccaneering old Gladstone', was by birth a Frenchman.

This traffic in men and ideas, however, was not all in one direction. Even Norman building became Anglo-Norman. The rib-vaults of Durham cathedral (which was begun in 1093 and completed forty years later) were the earliest in Europe. The ornamentation of twelfth-century churches, lavish by comparison with the bareness of the buildings of the first generation, included some motives which probably took their rise in England (the chevron ornament, for example). It is even possible that the Anglo-Norman style was exercising some influence upon church building upon the opposite side of the Channel by the early years of the twelfth century. In a like manner, it is also possible that some Englishmen were making their contribution to the ferment of ideas of the time. One example illustrates the new opportunities opened up by the Conquest and the use which might be made of them. Towards the end of the eleventh century we begin to hear of a man called Adelard of Bath. He tells us that he was an Englishman; though his west of England origin, his wanderlust and his individualism may suggest that there was Celtic blood in his veins. He was educated in the schools of central France, for he was an undergraduate at Tours and later a teacher at Laon (where more than one of the bishops and civil servants of twelfth-century England was trained). Whilst at Laon, he travelled to Spain and Italy and came into contact with Arab learning, which had preserved much of the science of ancient Greece. About 1109 he decided to extend the scope of his investigations, and for seven years travelled extensively in Asia Minor, Palestine and Syria. One result of these travels was his translation into Latin of an Arabic version of Euclid's *Principles of Geometry*, which he made available for the first time to the western world. After all this adventure, he may have ended his life a civil servant; but he was not without appreciation of proper recreation. He also wrote a treatise on falconry, the sport of kings.

This quickening of the contacts between England and the continent which followed the Conquest was something which lasted. The twelfth and thirteenth centuries were a time of international churchmen, knights errant, and wandering scholars; and England became part of their province. It received Cistercians and Franciscans from Europe. It sent St. Thomas Becket to acquire book-learning in Paris and a stream of budding archdeacons to study law in Bologna; while Stephen Langton had been a distinguished teacher in the Parisian schools before he came home as Archbishop of Canterbury and one of the framers of Magna Carta. Even William Marshall—tutor to Henry II's son, a diplomat for Richard I and regent in the early years of Henry III—had won his reputation as a professional jouster in all the tournaments of western Europe. Before the modern nations had emerged England had been absorbed into, and made some contribution to, the medieval civilisation of the west. For all their nearness to the barbarian strain in the western order, the Normans played a great part in making this possible.

IV

Underneath this interplay of ideas and artistic impulses, of course, everyday life went on; and here there may have been relatively little change. The growing towns may have received a stimulus from closer commercial contact with the continent, and a few Frenchmen might settle in the boroughs. Yet William the Conqueror quite naturally addressed the Londoners, in his charter to the city, in the Saxon tongue; and when a great Belgian scholar sought a representative type for the early medieval merchant, he found him in a post-Conquest Englishman, Godric of Finchale. His is the typical medieval success story. Starting life as a pedlar, he became a great exporting merchant before, repenting of his economic virtues, he took refuge in a hermitage and ended as a saint. In this connection, it may even be remarked that (though Thomas Becket's father might have done so) it would hardly be regarded as proper for a Norman to turn to trade. The majority must have settled down as gentlemen, and in the twelfth century a civil servant already gives expression to a familiar sentiment: 'If a knight or other freeman should so far demean himself (which God forbid) as to acquire money by engaging in trade, . . .' he begins. Trade, in short, was a vocation on the whole proper only to Saxons who, before the Conquest, had envisaged the possibility of a trader prospering into the aristocracy. Doubtless it is the Saxon heritage that has made us a nation of shopkeepers.

In the countryside, too, the Saxons remained the hewers of wood and drawers of water. Norman lords took over the ownership of the villages where they lived, and even gave those villages new christian names as at Helion Bumpstead, Hatfield Peverel, Woodham Ferrers and Berners Roding. But agricultural routine continued to be the lot of the Englishman, directed often by an English overseer. Sometimes we even catch glimpses of these peasants still pushing forward the boundaries of cultivation with little or no reference to their overlords. Such were the men who, in the middle of the twelfth century, gave little parcels of land to Thorney Abbey in the fields they had reclaimed from the fens on the borders of Lincolnshire and Cambridgeshire. Their names are eloquent of their Saxon or Scandanavian descent: Wigan the son of Landri, Thurstan, Alward of Wisbech, Godric the knight, Estan, Sunmard. They were merely carrying on the work of those generations of English pioneers who, before 1066, had created most of the English villages we know to-day and some others that had disappeared under sheep-runs by the time the Reformation came to England.

So much continuity there was; but there was also significant change. In the upper ranks of society, indeed, there was something of a social revolution. The Old English aristocracy disappeared: some into exile in Ireland or Scotland, some into the ranks of the Varangian guards in Constantinople, and many dead in the battles and revolts of the years round 1066. The possessions, and above all the landed possessions, of this old aristocracy were parcelled out amongst the leaders of the Norman army of occupation. The king kept a good deal; the rest was distributed to a narrow circle of great lay magnates, great bishops and great abbots. In return these great barons, as they were called, were required to provide quotas of troops for the king's army and for garrisoning castles. The barons in turn, therefore, commonly maintained the troops they required by sub-allotting part of their lands to knights —the mounted soldiers who provided the main striking force of the Norman army. These arrangements, characteristic of the so-called feudal system which the Normans had known at home, were a practical method of maintaining and keeping in being the Norman army of occupation. The feudalisation of England by the Conqueror and his companions was the outcome of the need to provision and equip a standing army.

Yet if the land-settlement of the Norman Conquest arose out of the practical requirements of the military situation, its long-term consequences were of a different order. In the long run, the Conquest gave England a small, compact, close-knit aristocracy, possessing vast wealth and vested interests worth defending even against the king who had created them. The greater baronage, therefore, very soon became defenders of private rights against governmental interference. As early as 1100, they exacted from Henry I promises that he would restrict the exercise of his royal office within boundaries defined by equity and fair-dealing. Henry broke the promises he made, but they had been set down in writing in his coronation charter. That charter was produced when Stephen Langton and King John's barons extorted Magna Carta from the king; and Magna Carta enshrines the principle that the power of the ruler to infringe private rights is limited by rules of law. This principle has never quite ceased to operate, even under the Tudors; and that 'good, old decrepit law of Magna Carta', exacted by the feudal aristocracy from a medieval king, has played its part in keeping it alive.

While the barons were becoming politicians, the knights too were changing their character. Within a hundred years of the Conquest many of them were ceasing to be fighting men and were being called, rather disparagingly, 'rustic knights'. They were settling down in their shires and taking up the tradition, established in pre-Conquest times, that the local man of substance bore a heavy responsibility in local affairs. They were becoming, in fact, country gentlemen, and playing a great part in local government as sheriffs and coroners; they shared in the work of juries and royal commissions of enquiry. Later still, in the fourteenth century, it was natural to find such men on commissions of the peace; and in such a capacity their descendants continued to serve for many centuries. In these ways the gentry acquired a training in public affairs which, from the time of Montfort and Edward I, took them to parliament as the leading members of what became the house of commons. There, in the seventeenth century, they in turn became the defenders of the principles of Magna Carta. They took over from the baronage the rôle of defending private rights, and finally subjugated the monarchy. In that long evolution they soon lost any resemblance to the professional cavalrymen of the Conquest. A knight became merely an honourable sort of gentleman, and there is nothing military about a gentleman as he is described by Sir Thomas Smith in the sixteenth century:

As for gentlemen (he wrote) they be made good cheap in England. For whosoever studieth the laws of the realm, who studieth in the universities, who professeth liberal sciences and, to be short, who can live idly and without manual labour, and will bear the . . . charge and countenance of a gentleman, he will be taken for a gentleman.

This was the end of a long road; but it began when the cavalrymen of the Conquest were endowed with land, and gradually assumed the attitudes and the responsibilities which went with the possession of land.

V

The social changes which followed the Conquest, therefore, created two important advocates of the rights of the subject during the middle ages and beyond. The Conquest, however, also augmented the power and authority of another participant upon the constitutional and political field—the medieval monarchy. And here it may be appropriate to complete that passage from Sir Frank Stenton's book which was quoted earlier. 'The Normans were closest of all the western peoples to the barbarian strain', you will remember; but he goes on, 'Politically they were the masters of their world'. This mastery of medieval arts of governance, which they showed also in Normandy and Sicily, the Normans developed most fully in England. It was not an achievement that was solely the work of kings. At its best it was perhaps the common achievement of kings and nobles co-operating in the common council of the realm, in the shires and in the baronies. There were times, many times, when one partner or the other transgressed against the dictates of discretion or the common estimate of right conduct. It was on such occasions that the aristocracy stood forward as defenders of private rights, or the monarchy as the champion of equity and order and discipline. The importance of the aristocratic movement has already received discussion; but the contribution of the monarchy to medieval social and political order is hardly of less importance.

When William of Normandy came to England, he assumed with his crown an office already invested with high powers and heavy responsibility by the West Saxon house which produced Alfred and Athelstan and

Edgar. To this tradition William added his personal contribution. We know something of the external man from William of Malmesbury's chronicle:

> He was of moderate height, immense corpulence, fierce countenance, going rather bald in front; of such strength of arm . . . that no-one was able to bend the bow which he himself could draw when his horse was at full gallop. He was a man of the greatest dignity whether sitting or standing, despite the deformity of a protruding stomach.

Bald and corpulent though he might be, however, he managed to impose, always with vigour and sometimes with violence, a strong kingship upon his army and his conquered realm. Even a Saxon could appreciate some of the benefits this entailed, as the chronicler did who wrote these words:

> The king William, about whom we speak, was a very wise man and very powerful, more dignified and strong than any of his predecessors were. He was mild to the good men who loved God; and over all measure severe to the men who gainsaid his will. . . . No-one durst do anything against his will. He had earls in his bonds who had acted against his will; bishops he cast from their bishoprics and abbots from their abbacies, and nobles into prison. . . . Among other things is not to be forgotten the good peace that he made in this land, so that a man . . . might go over his realm unhurt with his bosom full of gold. Nor durst any man slay another man, had he never so much evil done to him. He truly reigned over England.

Men grumbled about William's rule. There were the castles he made them build and the taxes he made them pay. 'He loved the tall red deer as if he were their father', and this made him unsympathetic to poaching, the age-old hobby of the villager. Nevertheless, he truly reigned over England. He made good peace in the land, a rare commodity in the Europe of his day.

This personal achievement of the Conqueror's survived him. There were men amongst his successors, like Rufus, who 'feared God but little and man not at all'; or like Stephen, a good soldier 'but in other respects practically an idiot'. But there were also others—Henry I, with his gifts for administration; Henry II, with his taste for law and a personality no less strong than the Conqueror's; and Edward I, whose character exhibited so many of the qualities which enabled the medieval English monarchy to count upon the respect and co-operation of its subjects. Under William I kingship perhaps demanded, in the main, a personal tour de force on the king's part; but owing not a little to his work and character, as well as to the achievements of some of his great successors, modification and refinement were introduced. Royal powers were delegated to administrative institutions, which made government more orderly, more regular and less capricious. The temptation of power to run into license was confined by rules of law and right governance, accepted by kings with a strong sense of their responsibilities and defended by subjects with as strong a sense of their rights. Kings could still be tyrants and subjects factious; but very much of the strength and toughness of the medieval English polity goes back to the monarchy which William I created out of Anglo-Saxon precedent, to his control over Norman force, and to his own indomitable personality. It was this monarchy which in medieval times completed the unification of England; gave the land good peace, a common law and common ordered government; and soon obliterated the distinction between conquered Saxons and Norman conquerors, so that only Englishmen remained.

In all that has been said in these pages, it has not been easy (if it is possible at all) to isolate and define the Norman heritage. It is true that some portions of their bare, undecorated churches can still be seen, though much built over in other styles. Some portions of their castles still remain; but these too have often been rebuilt or allowed to moulder away into grass-covered mounds. There is, moreover, far less Norman blood in English veins than our aristocracy has some-times liked to pretend. Part of the difficulty, indeed, of isolating the Norman heritage may be due in the last resort to the fact that they were an adaptable people. In England and in Sicily the tale is the same, despite the marked differences of environment. They took over much that was indigenous, learnt from the conquered and from anyone else who would teach them. Apart from anything else, therefore, we owe to the Normans the transmission of large parts of the Saxon heritage: villages and towns, parishes and shires, traditions of monarchy, the basic structure of our language.

Yet they also added something of their own. They brought England closer to the continent at a vital period, and enabled Englishmen to play a part in the ferment of that time. They settled the social structure of English society in its upper ranges for centuries, and helped to create social attitudes which have an even longer history. They gave a direction to English constitutional development no less long-lived—so much so that, however new the issues were, royalists and puritans in the seventeenth century were still arguing out their problems in the light of precedents drawn from the Middle Ages. Even so, and even in these respects, it is still not easy to separate out the specifically Norman share in the heritage of early Britain from that which was older and accepted by them. More than that, even where they would appear to have been innovators, they were still accommodating and still willing to use the services of others to their ends. We cannot really analyse the heritage of early Britain as if it was a chemical compound. Part of the Norman share of it is their transmission of the Saxon heritage; a great deal that we might at the first glance call Norman may have been the work of Frenchmen or Italians or even Englishmen. But perhaps the last word here belongs to Archdeacon Humphrey Hody:

> What does it matter to us who are descended, not only from those that are supposed to have been conquered, but also from their conquerors; and are the heirs and inheritors of all their rights and liberties?

SUGGESTIONS FOR FURTHER READING

F. M. Stenton, *Anglo-Saxon England*, 1943, 2nd ed. 1947.

F. M. Stenton, *William the Conqueror* (Heroes of the Nations Series), 1908.

F. M. Stenton, *The First Century of English Feudalism, 1066–1166*, 1932.

F. W. Maitland, *Domesday Book and Beyond*, 1897.

F. M. Powicke, *Medieval England* (Home University Library), 1931.

A. W. Clapham, *Romanesque Architecture in England* (The British Council, Arts in Britain Series), 1950.

A. W. Clapham, *Romanesque Architecture in Western Europe*, 1936.

The Anglo-Saxon Chronicle. (The cheapest translation of a version of the *Chronicle* is that of J. Ingram in Everyman's Library.)

VIII

DAVID KNOWLES

The Heritage Completed

IN the series of lectures from which this book took its rise it was the task of the last speaker to gather up the threads, to adjust the focus of the glass, and to show something of a pattern where his predecessors had shown details. In a book this is no longer necessary. The writers have seen each other's work and have been able to remove all discordancies that were not the expression of deliberate differences of opinion; the reader, unlike the audience of a weekly lecture, remembers what he has recently read or, if he forgets, has but to turn the pages. In a sense, therefore, there is no need for a last chapter; the writer on the Normans has taken the story to the threshold of English history and English literature—the literature and history of the modern English nation. Nevertheless, the previous chapters have been almost entirely self-contained, looking backward or forward scarcely at all, and there may still be room for a wider glance.

Now it is certainly very dangerous to press too closely the analogy between the life of an individual and the life of a nation. In the one, the thinking, acting personality gives a true unity to the career: in the other, the only unity is that imposed upon events by minds that look back on the past. Yet the analogy is there, however remote. A nation of the modern world, like the individuals composing it, has its racial ancestry, its parents, its pre-natal history, its impressionable infancy, its childhood of experience, its adolescence with its vivid emotions and its eager appreciations and debates, its conscious attempts to make its own character and fortunes. Far behind us, it seems, yet only yesterday in the duration of the world, are the simple but necessary discoveries, common now to all the human race, but made, some of them, thousands of years ago for us in this island—the elementary technique of cooking, of hunting, of ploughing, of the skilful use of the rudest of tools, of the domesticating of animals. And at the same time there was the crossing of blood and the adaptation to a climate. Time, like space, has its foreshortenings. It is difficult to realise that the same space of time separated Henry I from Henry VIII as separates Henry VIII from George VI, or that the landing of William I is nearer to us in time than was the landing of Cæsar to him. We find it harder still, even with all the helps of archæology, to realise the thousands of years that passed while men lived in England, in the caves of Derbyshire and Somerset, leaving neither monuments nor records. Yet these thousands of years seemed long enough to the men and women who then were alive—the generations that appear to us, as they appeared to Homer and the Psalmist, to fall like summer grass or autumn leaves.

Then there are the more direct influences: the Celtic, Belgic and Roman improvements in agriculture; the beginnings of national crafts and industries—fishing, weaving, mining, pottery, and the first knitting of the bonds of trade with the continent, with the Mediterranean and with the northern islands—the export of tin and hides, the import of weapons and amber. And then, still pre-natal to the English nation, the framework of Roman Britain and the window opened upon the wide landscape of the ancient civilisation. Then at last, in the centuries between the departure of the legions and the coming of the knights, the infancy and childhood of the English people, now at last our recognisable kith and kin; and then the Norman Conquest, with its stresses and its following flood of social and intellectual awakening, like the rough first days of life at a boarding-school, followed by the new horizons and deep loyalties of school life. All this, perhaps, may seem fanciful, yet it may help us to assess the many varying strata of our heritage.

If the chapters of this book convey anything of the picture that they gave when they were lectures, two very deep and lasting impressions will, I think, result from them. The first is—how little significance the English Channel had until the later centuries of the medieval period! Indeed, paradoxically enough, the further you go back the less is the Channel a barrier, until, if you go back far enough, it ceases to exist in physical fact. Certainly England, at least till the early years of the reign of Henry III, was at many moments, even of her historical life, more closely a part of Europe than she has ever been since. And you have to wait till the Reformation and the Spanish menace before you find an Englishman who thinks of his land as:

> This precious stone set in the silver sea
> Which serves it in the office of a wall,
> Or as a moat defensive to a house.

The second deep impression has already been hinted at: it is a new realisation of what one of the writers has called our mixed, mongrel breed. That, I think, has been made clear by all those who have written here, and especially by the archæologists. Our daily life still abounds in commonplace evidence of this. Our names for days and months and seasons, our method of reckoning dates, the names of our mountains, rivers and villages, all tell the same tale. It is not difficult in a train or road journey of sixty miles or so to recognise the place-names of five or more peoples. Ashby-de-la-Zouch in Leicestershire is about that distance from the ridge of Caer Caradoc in Shropshire, and between them lie Coventry and Worcester, to say nothing of the hamlet of Wixford, that preserves a people's name.

In the first two chapters we were brought very near to our remote ancestors and their works, so primitive and yet so impressive. Sometimes, as in the hills about Edinburgh, one age joins another in oblivion:

> Grey recumbent tombs of the dead in desert places,
>   Standing stones on the vacant wine-red places,
> Hills of sheep and the howes of the silent vanished races.

These, like Keats' Grecian Urn, can 'tease us out of thought as doth eternity'. And when we cease to be pure archæologists, when we look at the flint mines of Grimes Graves, with the disused antlers and the smoke-stained roof, or when we marvel at the stones of Avebury and the hill of Cissbury, we feel also that these things could not have been achieved without very elaborate organisation and a very perfect technique. Avebury and Stonehenge rouse perhaps still deeper thoughts. These monuments have a grandeur of scale and an evidence of purpose that takes them into the realm of the sublime. For what end were they constructed?

M

We do not know; they antedate both history and letters. But we should think seriously before we dismiss such a people as barbarous. Could the men who planned and built Avebury and Stonehenge have been devoid of emotions and sensibilities and imaginations as keen as ours?

Certainly as we draw nearer to the limits of pre-history we become less and less able to despise our ancestors. No one can look at the masterpieces—which after all are the accidental survivals—of La Tène art without a vivid sense that in exquisite freedom, together with balance in design, these Celtic artists have never been surpassed. If we look at them still more closely we shall find that artists in Britain had their own contribution to make both to Celtic design and Celtic technique. Indeed, when we look at these superb examples of art—and at the later Celtic master-pieces such as the Book of Kells, to which many expert critics would now give a provenance on this side of the Irish Channel—we feel that the word 'heritage' has almost a mocking ring. We have these precious things in our museums, but how can it be said that our crafts-men and designers have inherited anything so magnificent? Where is the heritage in our houses and streets?

And then we come to Roman Britain. That period of history has been washed, polished and ticketed by generations of experts. It has attracted scholars steeped in the literature and records of ancient Rome, and from the days of Camden, if not earlier, it has been the first love of English antiquaries. It may, however, be worth while to recall two aspects that are often neglected: the influence of Rome upon the population beneath, which never became Roman, and the legacy

of Christianity to the Celts, from which the marvellous
flower of early Irish culture sprang. I have heard an
eminent economist speak of the Roman occupation of
Britain as a mere scratch on the surface; he compared
it with the British Raj in India as seen by Indians two
thousand years hence. The comparison is a stimulating
one, but is it valid? We do not know what will be the
emotions of an Indian centuries hence when he
excavates the site of a British cantonment. We do not
know how many Indians then will owe their Christian
faith to European evangelisation. But we do know
that had there been no Romans in Britain our ancestors
of the Dark and Middle Ages would never have looked
back in quite the way they did, with a kind of nostalgic
pride, to the Roman Empire and to the Roman
civilisation. 'We too were Romans once', they said
again and again in one form of words or another, and
we echo the same tale. 'The Romans have been here',
we say, as we gaze at the line of a Roman road or the
traces of a camp in a pass of the mountains; or, on
Wenlock Edge, 'Then, 'twas the Roman; now, 'tis I'.
After all, there are surely two great differences between
British India and Roman Britain—first, the Indian
sub-continent had a long history of a series of highly
developed civilisations before John Company arrived,
and secondly, neither England nor all Europe can ever
be to India what Latin civilisation has been to north-
western Europe—not only a fountainhead in itself, but
the vehicle that has transmitted almost all that we
have of religion, and a fair half of what we have of
beauty.

Can we say the same of Celtic civilisation, of which
one chapter in this book has given such an unforgettable
picture? For better or worse, probably not. It may

M*

be that our heritage would be the richer for the purity of sentiment and the brilliance of hue, and the simplicity and spirituality of outlook of which we have read—the washed air and the incredible colours of flowers and sea and sky that surround Iona in July—but these are as little a part of the historic heritage of England (as distinct from Great Britain) as are the cliffs and misty lakes, the gnarled rowans and the strange monsters, that early English poetry inherited from Scandinavia. And if we ask how much Celtic blood we natives of England, who are not demonstrably of Welsh or Irish ancestry, have in our veins, the answer depends upon circumstances of which historians cannot be certain— the proportion of the Celtic population killed or exiled, the number of womenfolk brought over by the Saxons and Scandinavians when each group of invaders was firmly established on the land.

But before we leave the thought of Rome, it may be well to acknowledge our debt for the material legacy which the legions and administrators did not take with them when they left Britain to its fate. The Romans, like the English in modern times, carried with them more than their army and their trade; they took, or they had brought to them in their villas, the trees and the fruits, the birds and the animals, that seemed part of a civilised life in Italy. The pheasant and the cat, the cultivated rose that Vergil and Horace knew, the cherry and perhaps the pear were not all that they gave to Britain. This island, at the opening of history, was notably poor in the number of its trees and shrubs. The chestnut and walnut almost certainly, the elm and the beech possibly, were first seen in Roman times in the regions where villas clustered in Kent and Sussex and Gloucestershire.

And so we come to the Anglo-Saxons. Here for the first time we recognise our own features in our forebears. In Bede the Venerable, in Alfred the Great, in Dunstan of Canterbury, in Wulfstan of Worcester we see something that is familiar, something that is of home. We have from that age many elements of our heritage; among them are two that are all too little known. The Old English literature attained a subtlety, a range and a richness which no other European language of the time could rival. That is a heritage which we only enjoy in part. The English language did not develop and grow richer by steady progress. The Normans brought their own tongue with them, and they brought also with them the lettered monks and clerks who wrote in Latin. English, driven from court, survived only in common speech and perhaps in simple devotional books. Nevertheless, a multitude of our common names for things—and for flowers, birds, trees, vegetables and the implements of rural life—were in everyday use among the contemporaries of Alfred and Athelstan.

The second element of our Saxon heritage that deserves a wider enjoyment is Old English art. Though almost entirely small-scale, at least in southern England (and the sculpture of the northern crosses is earlier in time than the art of which we are speaking), and though it was very perishable by reason of the fragility and price of its media, it had a beauty and a delicacy far surpassing anything that came out of Normandy. The carved ivories, the remnants of jewellery and needle-work, and above all the line drawings of the illuminated manuscripts, are among the most beautiful works of art that western Europe produced between the age of Charlemagne and that of William the Conqueror.

Unlike the English language, English art, and especially the book-painting of the cloister, remained living during the early decades of the Norman plantation and helped to form the new style of the generations that followed. Indeed, one particular branch of the art—the animated illustrative drawings that appear in their most striking form in the copies of the so-called Utrecht Psalter— influenced a number of talented artists among the Anglo-Norman monks and continued in one form or another to reappear throughout the Middle Ages and beyond. Beyond, and into modern times, for Rowland- son probably, and Blake certainly, were directly inspired by some of the manuscripts now in the national collections.

In two earlier chapters, and in different contexts, it has been remarked that the map of rural England, at least east of the Pennines and south of the Mersey, was drawn by the Old English before the Conquest. The shires, save for the adjustments of modern administra- tion, remain almost exactly what they were on the day when King Edward was alive and dead; the villages bear the same names; even the fields and brooks were named then by the names still often known only to the farmer and the village children.

There is another sphere in which the Old English imprint lingers. The parochialisation of England is a thorny subject; its exact date, or rather the area of its extension at an exact early date, cannot be precisely fixed, but it is probably not too much to say that the greater part of the then inhabited portions of England (excluding, that is to say, the great tracts of forest, fen, moor and heath) was divided, if not into formal parishes, yet into areas depending upon, and paying dues to, a resident rural priest.

Certainly, in many country districts you may still travel long before you come across a village church standing on a site where no church stood in the days of Edward the Confessor. Not infrequently, the hamlet, until within living memory, was a recognisable descendant of its Domesday namesake, with church, mill and half-a-dozen cottages in the fields. The water-mill and the eel-trap, heritages from the Dark Ages, and the plough, derived in the main from the Celts, together with the ford which often gave the place its name, have disappeared since the present writer's childhood under the stress of steam and oil, but a church remains, though rarely with Old English stones, at the centre of a web of footpaths.

Another heritage, also ecclesiastical, has had a powerful influence of a different kind. The association of ecclesiastical and lay magnates under the King in the Witan, added to the practice of private ownership of churches, led to an intermingling of clerical and lay lawgiving and administration without a parallel in the Europe of the tenth and eleventh centuries. It was an intermingling that had grown and had not been devised; it begged no questions and led to no conflict of powers; seen in its historical setting it appears the most natural state of things in the world. In the event, however, it was to be treated as a precedent in more sophisticated days, when new problems and new demands had arisen, and some of the remote consequences of that intermingling are with us to-day.

And now, at last, for the Normans. We have been told that the original invaders were only some five thousand strong, and that of these by no means all were Normans. It is also true that the Normans themselves were racially not far distant from many of

the inhabitants of Cumberland and Yorkshire.   There
are becs in Normandy and becks in Yorkshire, 'and
there is trouts in both'.   And yet the Normans were
more foreign than the Scandinavians who came straight
from the North—partly because, in their short stay in
Normandy, they had absorbed with remarkable
adaptability the institutions of those they supplanted;
partly because, unlike other invaders from the North,
they came as a warrior aristocracy, with a talent for
domination and organisation greater than anything
that had been seen in the West since the palmy days
of Rome.   We must remember, also, that for fifty
years and more after the Conquest there was a steady,
if small, infiltration of Normans and others and—still
more important—that for almost 150 years after the
Conquest there was a stream, a thin stream, it is true,
but one socially, intellectually and politically important,
of bishops, abbots, barons and administrators from
Normandy, France and Italy.   It is not until the days
of Stephen Langton and Grosseteste that a wholly
English episcopate begins to consolidate, and not till
the death of Henry III that the higher baronage
becomes firmly and finally British.

In the chapter preceding this something was said of
Norman architecture.   That something was not wholly
complimentary.   The Normans from the beginning
planned churches on the grand scale and got them up
more quickly than we can do, but the construction was
poor, there was no finish to them, and the decoration
was scanty and barbarous for fifty years.   But whatever
may be thought of their architectural gifts, they were
certainly great builders.   They had a sense of size
and space;   they would have agreed with Aristotle
that a stature, a greatness, though not in itself beautiful,

is an essential ingredient of the highest forms of beauty. It was they who created and standardised the plan of the great church, and some of their buildings—Durham, Winchester, St. Albans, Ely—still remain among the largest, or at least the longest, churches of Europe.

We should certainly not be right in minimising or regretting the Norman Conquest, whatever sympathies or affinities may draw us to the Saxons. When all reserves are made and exaggerations avoided it still appears as a wholly decisive and, on the balance, undoubtedly beneficial change in the course of British history. The Normans were an extraordinarily energetic race, and in England, at least, guided by the Conqueror, they showed powers of organisation and initiative at every level that gave to both Church and State a method and a drive superior to that in any continental country. The Norman characteristics of restless energy and magnificence of planning exactly compensated the small-scale outlook and the static behaviour of the English, while their hard, unsympathetic, metallic make-up was refined by contact and admixture with the gentler, sweeter and more sensitive characteristics which, along with a good deal of boorishness and stupidity, were to be found in the higher ranks of the English.

But even more important than these assets was the opening upon Britain of the floodgates of European culture and institutions. The revival of learning, the revival of monasticism, the links with the reformed papacy, the invasion of canon law, and, in due time, the arrival of the university movement and of thirteenth-century theology and philosophy and science, and, later still, the contact with France and Italy that made up half of Chaucer's poetry—all these were in varying degree direct results of the Norman Conquest. Had it never taken place, it is at least possible, if not probable, that England would have become definitely a part of the northern, Scandinavian world, with what consequences it is as impossible as it is unprofitable to imagine.

Much has been said, in Chapter VII, of the social and institutional heritage of the Normans. They left their impress also on the organisation of the Church. The Conqueror, in the first place, carried through the last wholesale re-arrangement of the English bishoprics that was to take place till the age of Henry VIII. In his day· also, under Lanfranc and his immediate successors, the diocesan organisation began to function with the organs and officials that have survived all subsequent revolutions—the archdeacon, the diocesan synod, the chapter of the cathedral with its dean, precentor and the rest. Above all, it was the Norman kings and barons, with plenty of land to spare, who founded and endowed so lavishly the monasteries of monks and canons. There were some forty in existence in 1066. A century later the number was near three hundred. England no longer has the monastic life as a heritage of the Middle Ages, but she still has the monastic ruins as a heritage of beauty and as silent witnesses of the power of spiritual forces and of the infirmity of man's purpose.

The Normans, who changed so greatly the face of England with the garment of white churches of which an earlier French chronicler wrote, gave to the map of England (to use an anachronistic phrase) a pattern which was not to change greatly till the industrial revolution gave birth to new towns and villages by coalpits, canals and railways. William the Conqueror, by imposing the manorial organisation alongside, and sometimes cutting across, the casual grouping of village and hamlet, created the need—intensified by the swift expansion of the area of cultivation—of distinguishing names for different collections of houses lying in one parochial area, and for new divisions of old villages. Hence the new Christian name or surname of so many place names that are Saxon or Danish in origin. Sometimes the division is between two monasteries that hold in a single parish—Abbots Salford, the property of Evesham; Salford Priors, the land of Worcester—sometimes between a church and a lay owner, as at Pillerton Priors and Pillerton Hersey; sometimes the division is multiple, as between Church Lench, Rous Lench, Sheriff's Lench and Atch Lench. A careful sweep over the map of the midland and western counties will reveal almost all the great Norman baronial families—Croome Dabitot, Aston Cantlow, Norton Fitzwarren, Berry Pomeroy—and all the great religious orders—Toller Monachorum, White Ladies Aston, Hinton Charterhouse, Whitchurch Canonicorum, Brewood Black Ladies, Temple Guiting, Grosmont. Even individual Norman abbeys have left their mark, as at Tooting Bec and Newington Longville. The Tudors and the Hanoverians with their aristocracies of Russell and Cavendish have left their stamp on the schools and streets and squares of our cities, but the country still preserves the heritage of the Normans.

The history of England, up to the middle of the thirteenth century, is largely the history of the invasion of the land by conquerors and by ideas. Twice a culture has come with a conquest, but whereas the Romans only gave in an attenuated form to relatively few the treasures of the ancient world, the Normans were carriers and heralds of a powerful new life that found everywhere ready acceptance. Historians of ideas and of civilisations will probably remain divided in their judgement of that culture. Was it the one authentic European culture, classical and Christian, or was it a diluted, canalised stream, made almost provincial in the feudalised Western Empire which identified itself with Christendom? Whatever its nature, it came to England and left its stamp upon us, a stamp that remains in spite of all the divisions and revolutions, political, social and religious of the modern world.

A nation, it has been said, is made up of men sharing the heroes and the traditions of a common past. Too little, perhaps, has hitherto been said in this book of the historians of early England. They are a remarkable series. No country of Europe can surpass or match them, and they make up a line in which the great ones look consciously back to their predecessors, and try to rival them. At their head stands Bede the Venerable, the father of English history and worthy to stand beside the greatest of any age and country, rising far above his world in serenity and sanity and sober criticism, yet typically English in his warmth of feeling, his gentleness of touch, his reverence for the past and the patriotism with which he, an untravelled monk of the North, makes his own the struggles and the achievements of his countrymen all over England. Second only to Bede must come Alfred the Great, a historian in his own right in the pictures he gives of his England, and a historian by proxy in his patronage (which may indeed have amounted to part-authorship) of the Anglo-Saxon Chronicle, that work of many hands, enshrining, along with fragments of noble poetry, so many memorable phrases and vivid passages of narrative and reflection. It has been quoted more than once, both explicitly and without remark, in earlier pages.

Such is our heritage of history from the Old English, revered by Normans and English alike after the Conquest, and developed by writers such as Eadmer of Canterbury, the confidant of Anselm, Symeon of Durham and William of Malmesbury, all of them monks. They were only the greatest of a multitude of biographers, chroniclers and annalists. When the series ended, shortly before the reign of Edward I, with Matthew Paris, England had to wait almost four hundred years, till the days of Raleigh and Bacon, before another such galaxy appeared.

As for great men who are also the heroes of legend, three names stand out from Saxon times: Bede and Alfred again, and St. Dunstan. It is interesting to compare them with the three who have always been the heroic figures of the hundred-odd years after the Conquest: the Conqueror himself, Thomas Becket and Richard the Lion Heart. There is no doubt which group is nearer in temper to those who are, we feel, the most typical of the best of modern England, yet Becket and King Richard, for all that historians have done to lower their stature, have throughout the ages appealed to something in Englishmen that the others did not satisfy. Three of the six are saints, and it is worth remarking that the Saxon and Norman centuries left England a rich heritage of admirable lives. There is, indeed, no figure with the magnitude of Bernard or the originality of Francis, but Bede and Thomas were in their different ways renowned throughout western Christendom, Wulfstan of Worcester can be taken in any age as the model of a pastoral bishop who spends his life in the cathedral close and the country lanes, and in Anselm of Aosta and Canterbury and Hugh of Avallon and Lincoln, England received the most precious instance of itself that one country of Europe could give to another.

And so, to continue the metaphor used on an earlier page, England (for it would no longer be correct to say Britain) achieved its adult personality. Almost all who have pondered over English medieval history would agree that towards the very end of the thirteenth century something took shape that was not there before, an English nation with characteristics and institutions which are recognisably ours. If a moment had to be fixed for the twenty-first birthday party, the most convenient date would probably be found to be early in the reign of Edward I, say about the year 1280, so as to lay no emphasis on any meeting of Parliament that modern constitutional historians tell us was not as significant as their predecessors had supposed. Strangely enough that great king, Edward I, though very little about him was English save his name (given him by a father who revered the Confessor and did so much to beautify the national church of England, Westminster Abbey), had much that was typically English in his character, and the country he ruled was in its parliament, its social classes, its towns, its universities and its churches—even in the beginnings of its trade and its adoption of the national weapon, the longbow— recognisably the England that continued to develop without cataclysmic social change till the mid-eighteenth century. Within a few years, the English language floods up like a tide, invading the courts of law, parliament and the palace, giving expression to the religious experience of Rolle and to the poetic experience of Langland. A few years more, and Chaucer will present a gallery of portraits of men and women who, though they wear costumes and follow vocations unfamiliar to us, are sisters and brothers of the men and women of Shakespeare and Dickens.

It was a little England that thus emerged: Normandy had gone and France was an enemy; Ireland lay in the mist, Wales was in arms, and Scotland was about to fall away. But the English had decided, so to say, how much of their heritage they would claim and how much they would discard. Henceforward, if we may over-simplify history and over-stress a metaphor, the heritage became an heirloom and no further legacies were received. Yet in another sense, the heritage of the past awaits every individual, and he can discover it for himself, ever new and ever growing. It has been the purpose of this book to suggest where he may begin his search.

Index

Plate 1.   Class A beaker from Little Downham, near Ely, with associated
flint dagger and scraper, jet button and ring.

in.

cm.

Plate 2. Class A, B and C beakers from Eriswell, Runcton Holme and Snailwell respectively.

Plate 3. Personal hoard from Downham Fen, Norfolk. Rapier, looped palstave and socketed sickle found together.

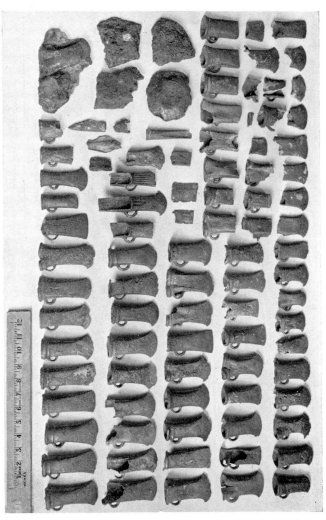

Plate 4.   Late Bronze Age Founder's Hoard from Stuntney Fen,
near Ely.

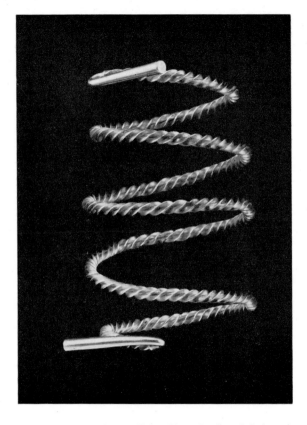

Plate 5. The Grunty Fen gold armlet (½ real size).

Plate 6. Creswell Crags, Derbyshire. Part of the northern side of the gorge, showing entrance to Mother Grundy's Parlour (Photo: A. L. Armstrong)

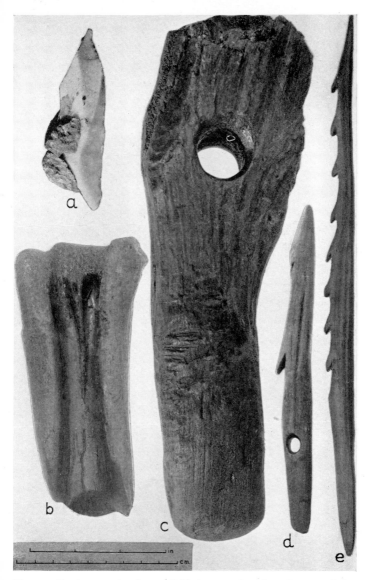

Plate 7. Equipment of early mesolithic hunters, Star Carr, Seamer, Yorks, shown at ½ real size, except (a) which is 1½ times real size.

(a) Microlith with portions of resin used for mounting. (b) Scraper made from metacarpal bone of wild ox. (c) Adze- or mattock-blade made from base of elk antler and adjacent bone. (d) Harpoon-head with hole for line made from red deer antler. (e) Barbed spear-head of red deer antler.

Plate 8.   Vertical air-photograph of 'Celtic' fields on
Windover Hill, near Eastbourne, Sussex.

[*Crown copyright reserved*]

Plate 9. Tasselled belt of horsehair of the
Late Bronze Age, from Armoy, County Antrim
(⅔ real size).

Plate 10. One of a pair of bronze flagons decorated with coral and enamel from Basse-Yutz, Lorraine. A masterpiece of La Tène Style I. The duck shows Hallstatt, the beasts oriental influence; the orm of the vessel is ultimately derived from the Etruscan beak flagon.

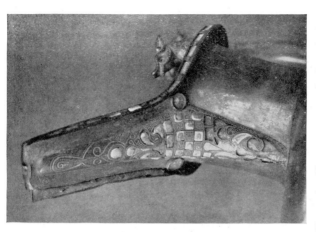

Plate 11a.   Detail from the flagon of Plate 10: the mask shows oriental influence.

Plate 11b.   The ornament at the flagon's throat is composed of classically derived motifs.

Plate 12a. Part of a bronze torc from the Marne. La Tène Style III, 'plastic substyle'.

Plate 12b. Bronze handle from a tankard, Trawsfynydd, North Wales, in the late 'boss-style'.

Plate 13*b*. Bronze scabbard from Hungary; Style III 'sword-substyle'.

Plate 13*a*. Part of a bronze sword scabbard from the Marne. The staple medallions bear Style II ornament; the sheath is decorated in Style III, 'sword-substyle'.

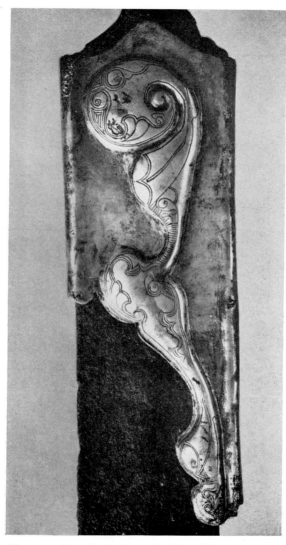

Plate 14. Sword locket from the River Witham. A fine
example of Style IV, the first British La Tène style.

Plate 15b. Ornament on a bronze crescentric plaque from Llyn Cerrig Bach, Anglesey.

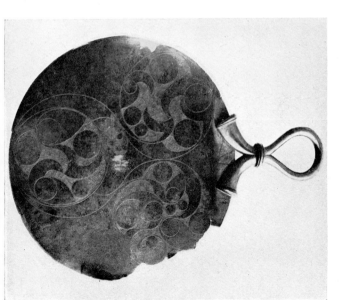

Plate 15a. British bronze mirror from the Mayer collection, Liverpool Museum, with ornament in the 'mirror style'.

Plate 16a. Bronze sacrificial dish from Ireland. Plate 16b. Bronze handle-escutcheon from Felmersham, Beds. This cow's head is an example of Belgic naturalistic art. Plate 16c. Enamelled bronze terret from Bapchild, Kent. Belgic work.

Plate 17. Hadrian's Wall, looking east from Cuddy's Crag. The ditch is on the left.

Plate 18.   A Roman road: the Fosse Way, looking north-east
towards Leicester from High Cross on Watling Street (Photo:
Dr. J. K. St. Joseph).

[*Air Ministry, Crown copyright reserved*]

Plate 19. Dunadd, Argyll, the earliest stronghold of the kings of Scotland.

Plate 20*a*.   Priestholm Island, near Anglesey, one of the
islands of the saints.

Plate 20*b*.   The Great Skellig Rock, Skellig Michael.   The
cross shows the site of the monastery.

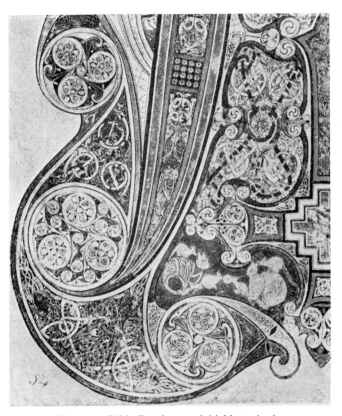

Plate 21.   Celtic Cats from an initial letter in the
Book of Kells.

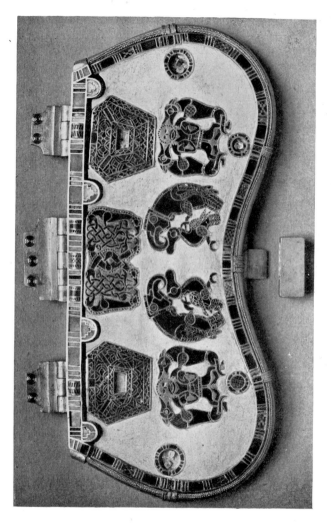

Plate 22. Jewelled Purse Lid from Sutton Hoo (⅔ real size).

Plate 23.   The Lindisfarne Gospels.   *St. Matthew*
chapter 1, verse 18.

Plate 24. A Seated Warrior of the 10th century, Nunburnholme, Yorkshire (Photo: T. Romans).